IN THE BEGINNING

A STUDY OF CREATION VERSUS
EVOLUTION FOR YOUNG PEOPLE

by

Rita Rhodes Ward

Illustrations by Charles Valentine

BAKER BOOK HOUSE
Grand Rapids, Michigan

PHOTOLITHOPRINTED BY CUSHING - MALLOY, INC.
ANN ARBOR, MICHIGAN, UNITED STATES OF AMERICA
1969

IN THE BEGINNING

TABLE OF CONTENTS

ACKNOWLEDGMENTS

The author wishes to express appreciation to the following companies for permission to quote from their publications: Baker Book House, Blaisdell Publishing Company, Columbia University Press, Concordia Publishing House, The John Day Company, Inc., DeHoff Publications, Doubleday & Company, Inc., E. P. Dutton & Co., Inc., Wm. B. Erdman's Publishing Co., Harper & Row, Publishers, Harvard University Press, D. C. Heath and Company, Holt, Rinehart and Winston, Inc., Alfred A. Knopf Incorporated, McGraw-Hill Book Company, Moody Press, W. B. Saunders Company, The University of Chicago Press, John Wiley & Sons, Inc., Publishers, Yale University Press.

Special thanks are due four men who read and criticized the manuscript. Dr. William J. Tinkle of Anderson College (retired), Eaton, Indiana, a geneticist of long experience, offered most helpful suggestions. As secretary of the Creation Research Society Dr. Tinkle is taking a leading part in refuting evolutionism. Valuable suggestions also were given by Dr. H. Douglas Dean, biology professor at George Pepperdine College. Dr. Dean did his graduate work in evolution so he might be prepared to refute the philosophy. Dr. George W. DeHoff, educator and author, offered encouraging remarks. The fourth critic was Mr. Robert Taylor who heads the church of Christ Bible Chair at the University of New Mexico, Las Cruces. Mr. Ronald T. Bailey of Sentinel Publishing Company rendered aid in setting up the format and the details of publication. This is much appreciated. Special thanks, also, are due Mr. Charles Valentine whose art work added so much to the attractiveness of the material. These men helped strengthen the work, but all faults must be the responsibility of the author.

Mrs. Mary Christian King, Secretary for the Montana Avenue Church of Christ, rendered valuable aid as a typist, and last but not least, many thanks to the elders of the Montana Avenue Church for the encouragement they have given me in this work.

PREFACE

This series of lessons was written that young people might have a basis for resisting evolutionary philosophy and holding firmly to their faith in God and the Bible. The book is being published at a time when public schools are being flooded with evolutionary teaching both in the classroom and in general reading. It is the hope of this writer that these lessons will help young Christians to resist that teaching.

TO THE TEACHER

Each of these lessons is complete as it is. There are questions to be answered and other suggested activities at the end of each lesson. It is not expected that the teacher will try to carry out all suggested activities. Some may not be practical for some teachers while other instructors may find them useful. The suggestions may stimulate thinking on the part of teacher and students and may lead to other ideas. Students should be encouraged to bring books and articles from periodicals and newspapers to class and discuss them. Class participation should be encouraged in every way possible.

The hard scientific facts that reveal the weaknesses in the theory are to be found largely in college, usually graduate, level books. The works students read seldom reveal those weaknesses. For this reason the references used in this production had to be works the student will not be able to read with profit.

The works listed as collateral reading on page 109 are by authors who believe in creation. They provide excellent background for the teacher, but most of them are more difficult than the student will care to read. These references have been carefully checked. However, the person who reads widely in this field soon learns that there are many variations of ideas among creationists. Even in this select list the reader may find ideas with which he does not agree or possibly errors may appear. Every effort was made to provide a list of works which are both scientifically sound and free of modernism.

Although these lessons are designed to show the fallacies in evolutionary philosophy and thus strengthen the student's faith, one should never forget that the real source of faith is the Bible itself. With this in mind appropriate scriptures are provided at the beginning of each lesson. Students should be encouraged to make them part of their Bible reading for the week.

LESSON 1

INTRODUCTION

The Bible is the inspired Word of God. Science is a search for the truth about the universe. Sometimes there are supposed contradictions between the Bible and science. This course is designed to show the student that the Bible is dependable and that the proposed theories of science that conflict with the Scripture have no valid basis.

Scripture: Heb. 11:1-39 "By faith we understand that the worlds have been framed by the word of God"; and like those of old we will keep that faith regardless of what others may say.

According to Raymond F. Surburg:

"An analysis of what human beings have written on the subject of origins shows that the ideas and speculations which have been expressed may be classified under two heads: (1) those that propose natural development and (2) those that ascribe the origins of the cosmos and of living creatures to divine creation." 1

The second belief, special creation, is based on faith in the Bible as an inspired book and acceptance of the brief account in Genesis. The Jews of earlier times as well as Christians later held to special creation. The belief was the accepted dogma of the Catholic church during the Middle Ages. The account in Genesis explains both the origin of matter, or the substances comprising the universe, and the origin of all living things, including man. Moses, in the book of Genesis, teaches that God created the universe but no explanation is made as to *how* the universe was created.

Most scientists accept evolutionary theory as offering the most plausible explanation of origins. There are two classes of evolutionists: organic and theistic. The organic evolutionist is entirely materialistic, usually atheistic. He makes no attempt to explain the origin of matter. He assumes its existence at the beginning of time. Beginning with this primeval some-thing — some say chemical elements while others begin with

4

energy — the evolutionists theorize that the stars evolved or formed, the earth was formed, and life appeared in some warm ocean and passed through successive stages until man appeared. The theistic evolutionist holds to similar ideas except that he believes in a god of some sort who created the original matter. Some theistic evolutionists believe God directed evolution while others believe He put the universe here, set up the natural laws, and then left nature to follow its course.

History of Evolutionary Theory

The definition of biological evolution as given by Webster's Unabridged Dictionary is as follows:

". . . the process by which, through a series of changes or steps, any living organism, or groups of organisms, has acquired the morphological and physiological characters which distinguish it; hence, the theory that the various types of animals and plants have their origin in pre-existing types, the distinguishable differences being due to modifications in successive generations." 2

According to this theory life began as minute living forms in some ocean. Some of these forms slowly changed becoming more complex and diversified until we have the present vast assemblage of plants and animals.

Moody presents a similar definition:

"For our purposes we define organic evolution as the theory that plants and animals now living are the modified descendents of somewhat different plants and animals which lived in times past. These ancestors, in their turn, are thought of as being the descendents of presuccessors which differed from them, and so on, step by step back to a beginning shrouded in mystery." 3

5

This definition leaves the impression that creationists admit no change since the beginning of time. This is not true. Scripture does not teach that species do not change and there is plenty of evidence of changes in the natural world but they are limited changes. Also, the definition does not present a complete definition of evolution as accepted by evolutionists of today. They believe all life started by natural means as extremely simple cells and progressed through successive stages from simple to complex, differentiating into many forms.

The idea that organisms (living things) have evolved or changed form is not a new one. Anaximander, sixth century B. C., Enophanes, sixth to fifth century B. C., and Empedocles, fifth century B. C., were three of the earliest Greek philosophers who expressed some idea of evolutionary theory. Aristotle, of the fourth century B. C. is more familiar to most students. He, too, believed in some sort of gradation though his theories were quite different from those of today. Count de Buffon (1707-1788), a Frenchman, can be called the father of modern evolutionary theory. Jean de Lamark (1744-1829), also French, proposed the theory that changes occurring in life, such as the loss of a limb by accident, are hereditary. Erasmus Darwin (1731-1802), the grandfather of Charles Darwin, believed in organic changes. A. G. Werner (1749-1817), a German, is famous for his "onion-coat" theory. He believed the rocks are arranged in definite strata (layers) in a specific order. The Englishman, William Smith (1769-1839) promulgated a similar idea substituting fossils for minerals. Baron Cuvier (1769-1832), a Frenchman, believed in a succession of local destruction of organisms which were replaced by migration from other regions. He was a creationist. Others of that time theorized a succession of cataclysmic destructions followed by re-creations. The Englishman, Sir Charles Lyell (1797-1875), was the father of modern historical geology. He rejected all idea of creation and had a great influence on Charles Darwin.

Count de Buffon 1707-1788	Called father of modern evolution. Expressed extensive evolutionary ideas in forty-four volumes of Natural History. French.
James Hutton 1726-1797	English geologist who developed the idea of uniformitarianism which is the basis of modern evolutionary geology. According to this theory all past geological changes were the same as those seen taking place today. "The present is key to the past."
Erasmas Darwin 1731-1802	Grandfather of Charles Darwin. Influenced his grandson with evolutionary ideas.
A.G. Werner 1749-1817	German famous for his "onion-coat" theory. Believed the strata of the earth occur in concentric shells.
William Smith 1769-1839	Taught fossils occur in definite strata or layers of definite order.
Baron Cuvier 1769-1832	Frenchman who believed different kinds of organisms were successively created and destroyed. This not true evolution.
Sir Charles Lyell 1797-1875	English geologist and friend of Darwin. Provided the foundation on which Darwin built. Was very influential.
Charles Darwin 1809-1882	Wrote ORIGIN OF SPECIES, a book which made evolution popular. Tried to explain the process as taking place through natural selection. Is credited with originating the theory of evolution but actually presented it to the public in such a way that it became widely accepted.

Chart No. 1

The most important name in the history of evolutionary thought is that of Charles Darwin (1809-1882). In the mind of the public he originated the idea, but as noted above he had a number of predecessors. His book, *The Origin of Species,* published in 1859, stirred up a tremendous amount of controversy and touched off the avalanche of evolutionary teaching which continues to this day. A fellow Englishman, Alfred Russell Wallace, proposed the same theory to Darwin in 1858. The two men presented their theory jointly to scientists in the Linnean Society in 1858. As a result of the publication of his book in 1859 Darwin's name became attached to evolutionary theory and Wallace is little known to the general public.

Contemporaries of Darwin who did much to promote the theory were the Englishmen, Thomas Henry Huxley (1825-1895) and Herbert Spencer (1820-1903) and the German, Ernst Heinrich Haekel (1834-1919). Since Darwin's day there has been a succession of scientists who aggressively teach the theory. This is not to imply that *all* scientists accept evolutionary hypothesis. Louis Agassiz and Henri Fabre are famous earlier scientists who were firm creationists, and there are many today, some in high position, who are creationists.

Kinds of Evidence

All evidence comes under one or the other of two classifications. *A priori* evidence is that based on reasoning alone. There is no way of demonstrating or proving by experimentation. *Empirical* evidence depends on experimentation. Mendel experimented with garden peas and determined from experimental evidence the basic principles of heredity. This is empirical evidence and his principles are called laws. To this date they have proven to hold true both for animals and for plants. The evolutionist uses a priori evidence when he observes the bones of the forelimbs of animals and concludes they have a common ancestor. The only way to prove a common ancestor would be to breed individuals for generations noting changes. This is impossible. All evidence for evolution is a priori.

Scientific evidence depends on man's knowledge and observation and thus is subject to error. Chemistry students were taught in pre-Einstein days that matter could be neither created nor destroyed. Today the atomic fission or the breaking of matter into other forms of matter plus energy is a common occurrence. The Law of Conservation of Matter had to be amended but its basic truth still holds true. Today it is stated: Matter and energy can be neither created nor destroyed. Converting matter into energy, as occurs in atomic fission, changes form but does not destroy.

Hypothesis, Theory, Law

These three terms are very important in the study of evolution. An hypothesis is a scientific idea for which there is very little evidence. With additional evidence a principle is called a theory while the principles for which there is conclusive evidence are called laws.

Most laws are in some way expressed in mathematical terms. Mendel's Laws of Heredity involve mathematical relationships. Theories often can not be so definitely stated as laws but they provide a working basis. The Atomic Theory is the basis of chemistry and physics. Many industrial processes are based on the Atomic Theory. The basic test of a good theory is its usability as a means of prediction. That is a theory concerning the nature of matter or energy can be used to predict nature or behavior under new circumstances.

Since atoms have not been seen but their properties have been inferred from other evidence, the principle is called a theory. Einstein used this theory to predict the type of explosion which occurs in the atomic bomb. On the basis of this prediction the bomb was constructed and its success proved the validity of Einstein's prediction.

An hypothesis may be no more than an idea or an assumption. There may be little or no evidence. The three terms overlap in many ways so it is impossible to draw a sharp line between them.

Evolution commonly is called a theory. Since so many theories such as the Atomic Theory and the Cell Theory are so well established that they are considered true, it is easy for the evolutionist to take one step further and assert evolution to be a fact. In reality there are so many weaknesses in the principle that it is no more than an hypothesis, and that is what it should be called.

No useful prediction has come from evolution. It is not the basis of any useful process. The closest one could get to using evolution as a basis of prediction is to predict changes in species or higher categories. As has been discussed previously, all observed changes are limited to the lower categories and can be explained on the basis of Mendel's Laws of Heredity. Thus evolution does not provide a basis for predicting possible future changes.

Some evolutionists say that the theory of evolution is to biology what the Atomic Theory is to the physical sciences. It can be seen from the above discussion that this claim is not true. The Atomic Theory can be verified by laboratory means and it is the basis of useful processes while evolutionary hypothesis can not be verified and is not used as a basis for industrial processes. It is not possible to draw a valid analogy between these two ideas.

How to Distinguish Fact From Theory

Since theory plays such an important part in the so-called conflict one would like to know how to distinguish fact from theory. With Man's imperfect knowledge that isn't always possible. Some scientific ideas previously thought to be undeniable fact are now questioned or even proven false. Scientists know these uncertainties and are careful to consider them.

On the writer's desk is a beautiful fossil shellfish from South Dakota. It is classified as an ammonite. It is approximately seven inches wide at its widest diameter and is flattened in shape. It is covered with a lovely pearly shell in hues of pink, pale green, and violet tones. These are all facts about the shell. There are no known ammonites in existence today. Since some parts of the sea may be unexplored there could be found ammonites yet but scientists would be just as surprised as they were when the coelocanth was discovered. It is assumed the shell is the original color, but can one prove the colors have not changed, perhaps faded some? Since ammonite shells closely resemble the shells of modern nautilus, it is assumed the animals were much like the nautilus. But since no living ammonite has been seen no one knows how the animal looked. The fossil came from rocks dated by geologists as Upper Cretaceous or about sixty-three million year old. The characteristics of the formation where the shell was found are known. That is a matter of observation. But the age of the formation is theoretical. There is no way to prove it.

From this brief discussion the difference between facts and theories can be seen. Facts can be observed or tested experimentally but theories are ideas about the facts. The facts are truth and can not conflict with scripture but theories sometimes do conflict. As we study these lessons we will see how evolutionists interpret facts from their own bias or point of view and we see that what often is treated as fact really is opinion about facts.

Why Christians Should Study About the Hypothesis

Most biologists consider evolution to be the unifying theme in biology. The theory is considered the foundation of modern natural science. Ruth Moore refers to the belief as, "that most basic of all the sciences, the evolution of man." 4

Moody well expresses the philosophy of a large number of the scientists of today:

"Organic evolution is the greatest general principle in biology. Its implications extend far beyond the confines of that science, ramifying into all phases of human life and activity. Accordingly, understanding of evolution should be part of the intellectual equipment of all educated persons." 5

Here Moody tells us that the theory is so important that it should be part of the education of all people. Since most biologists adhere to this philosophy it is to be expected that the theory will appear quite often in text books, and other reading, and in the class room as well. This proves to be the case. In a study made by the author of this work it was found that from ten to fifteen per cent of the biological material contacted by high school students is of an evolutionary nature. (See "Christian Bible Teacher," Oct. 1962) Recent text books contain a much higher amount of such teaching. Since the theory conflicts with the Bible, it is important that students become familiar with the theory and its relation to scripture.

The following objectives will be the basis of this course:

1. To learn something of what scripture does and does not teach regarding the creation and the flood.

2. To learn the basic principles of evolutionary theory.

3. To learn some of the scientific weaknesses in those principles.

4. To learn how to distinguish between evolutionary theory and fact.

5. To acquire a basic philosophy which will stabilize one's faith regardless of what theories may be taught.

SUGGESTED ACTIVITIES

1. Bring to class biology texts, library books, comic books, or any other books containing evolutionary teaching. List some of the ideas of evolution one can get from pictures or reading.

a. ....

b. ....

c. ....

2. Make a list of reasons why so many people accept evolution instead of believing the Bible.

a. _____

b. _____

c. _____

3. Give reasons why so often those who accept evolution are said to be intelligent or informed.

a. _____

b. _____

c. _____

4. List some reasons why Christians should study evolution.

a. _____

b. _____

c. _____

5. According to Moody an "understanding of evolution should be part of the intellectual equipment of all educated persons." Is an understanding synonymous with believing? Comment:

_____

_____

_____

_____

6. A class activity: Start a class collection of clippings from newspapers, magazines, etc. Mount them in a scrap book or post them on a bulletin board. List some ideas about evolutionary teaching one gets from such material.

a. _____

b. _____

c. _____

d. _____

REFERENCES

1. Zimmerman, Paul A. (Editor), *Darwin, Evolution and Creation,* "In the Beginning God Created", by Raymond F. Surburg, Concordia Publishing House, St. Louis, Missouri, 1959, p. 38.

2. Webster's *New International Dictionary,* Second Edition, Unabridged, G. C. Merriam, Springfield, Massachusetts, 1957.

3. Moody, Paul A., *Introduction to Evolution,* Second Edition, Harper and Brothers, New York, 1962, p. 1.

4. Moore, Ruth, *Man, Time, and Fossils,* Alfred A. Knope, New York, 1953, p. 3.

5. Moody, op. cit., p. ix.

LESSON 2
ORIGIN OF THE UNIVERSE

Scripture: Gen. 1:1-10; 14-19; Ps. 19:1-6 Truly the heavens declare the glory of God, for He created them.

In a few verses in Genesis 1 we have God's revelation of the creation of the universe. Many scientists discredit the inspiration of the Bible and attempt to explain the origin of matter and energy on a purely materialistic basis. In this lesson we shall examine the leading theories and contrast them with Genesis 1.

Origin of Matter

In Genesis 1 is found the simple account of the origin of the universe and of life. Verses 1-10 and 14-19 give us the origin of the non-living matter, its organization or arrangement, and the creation of light. Verses 11-13; 20-27 tell of the creation of living things. Details are omitted. The outstanding idea is that God is eternal and is the source of our universe—that He created both matter and energy from nothing. Hebrews 11:3. About seventy-five other references in the Bible refer in some way to God as the creator. The chaotic condition of the universe, the creation of light and of day and night, the separation of land and seas, and the creation of the heavenly bodies are described in mere skeleton outline. This is all God tells us. He created the materials and energy of the universe but He doesn't tell how He did it.

Philosophers and scientists offer no explanation as to the origin of matter. Pantheists consider God and the universe as one. Atheists say there is no God. Agnostics add, "We

13

have no evidence, therefore we don't know." Skeptics doubt God while infidels do not believe in God. Most scientists in describing the origin of the universe start with matter or energy or both already in existence. They make no attempt to explain their origins. They merely assume their existence. From that assumption they explain how the stars and planets were formed. However recent studies of the breakdown of radioactive elements force scientists to new conclusions. Note what Patrick M. Hurley has to say:

"The measurement of time by study of the continuous breakdown of radioactive elements has had great impact on science and philosophy. We have learned that the naturally occurring radioactive elements are constantly decreasing in a-bundance, and this phenomenon forces upon us a new realization. It demands a creation of these elements, and therefore probably of all elements, at some definite time in the not-too-distant past. The elements of the world we live in definitely were not in existence forever; therefore, neither was this earth, nor this solar system, nor our galaxy of stars." 1

This is an important admission from a scientist but we note he does not bring God into the picture. Hurley further says the following:

"It is almost incomprehensible that only a few billion years ago our galaxy was born in a giant bomb-flash of nuclear energy. What an inspiring picture of the process of creation." 2

Hurley does not explain the origin of the nuclear energy.

Rush also admits the failure of science to find the origin of matter:

"Let me say at once that we have no reason to believe we are any nearer to *the* beginning, the origin of all things— if such there was—than were our unscientific ancestors." 3

Origin of the Earth

Even though they don't explain the origin of energy or matter, evolutionary scientists try to explain the formation of the universe and the earth from that matter. The first theory regarding the origin of the solar system which attracted much attention was the nebular hypothesis of the Frenchman, Laplace. In 1796 Lap-lace proposed that a great cloud of gas rotated and as it did so it contracted. In the process rings of gas were thrown off, and they contracted to form the planets with their satellites. This hypothesis was generally accepted for about one hundred years. By 1859 J. C. Maxwell proved by theoretical means that planets could not have been formed from gaseous rings.

Nebular Hypothesis

The hypothesis of Chamberlin and Moulton replaced that of Laplace by 1900. These scientists proposed that a star came near the sun and by gravitation pulled off masses of matter which condensed into the planets. Henry Morris Russell explained that the passing star could not account for the extent of the angular momentum of the stars. Lyman Spitzer, Jr. proved that the sudden releasing of a mass at a temperature of a million degrees would result in its being exploded by its own radiation and it never could condense into a planet.

Chamberlin-Moulton Hypothesis

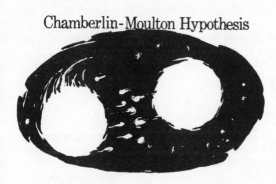

After the collapse of the Camberlin-Moulton proposal, a British scientist, Fred Hoyle theorized that the sun was once one of a pair or was part of a double star. The companion star exploded and formed the planets. The findings of Russel and Spitzer are against this proposal also.

Hoyle's Hypothesis

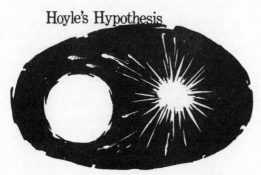

At the present several scientists are working on the theory that the entire solar system formed from a giant cloud of gas and dust within the galaxy. Most of the gas formed the sun while eddies formed the planets. They recognize weaknesses but hope to learn facts which will explain away the weaknesses.

Origin of the Universe

Theories about the origin of the earth, of course, can not be separated from theories concerned with the origin of the entire universe. There are two current theories about the origin of all matter.

According to the Superdense State Theory about six billion years ago all matter and energy were compressed into a very compact mass with very high temperature. The mass exploded and the original neutrons formed atoms, the atoms formed molecules, molecules formed masses of gas which condensed to form all the stars and planets. Experimental tests indicate the universe is presently expanding. Later there may be some means of confirming the age, and other tests may be made. It is evident the supporters of this theory do not account for the origin of the original mass. Scripture explains that.

The Steady State Theory takes a different approach. According to this theory hydrogen atoms are appearing in space at a constant rate which has been estimated at about 100 trillion tons per year. These atoms form clouds which successively change composition so that all the elements are formed. The clouds condense into the heavenly bodies which pass from telescopic view only to be replaced by newly created bodies. It is believed this has continued since infinity. Thus the universe is eternal. Scientists are divided in their acceptance of the theory.

Theories Compared with Scripture

Let us compare the Biblical account of the creation of the universe with these theories. The Bible merely teaches that God created but does not tell how He created. The theories begin with the substance of the universe already present and attempt to explain how the matter or energy was organized to form the solar system. But even if the scientists do deny God and try to explain all by purely natural laws they recognize some limitations and some facts that come close to scripture. Hurley admits that the radioactive processes point to a beginning. The Bible explains the beginning. Rush states that we have not come to "*the* beginning" of all things thus admitting that science does not explain the origin of the universe. Scripture simply states the source of the universe. Rush has this interesting statement:

"Several really startling findings in recent years point to the conclusion that our earth and the other planets and all the stars and other matter in the known universe came into being roughly at the same time, and that this time of vast beginnings was no more than four to six billion years ago." 4

 God merely tells us creation was "In the beginning." If scientists give satisfactory proof that the materials of the universe have been here four to six billion years will it be unscriptural to believe that? God did not explain how he organized the material into suns and planets. If scientists propose a method which will "hold water" scientifically, would it be unscriptural to accept their explanation?

Following a discussion of the possibility that the universe originated as the result of a giant nuclear explosion, Rush has this interesting comment:

"Yet no one should hasten to proclaim that this primeval cataclysm, if it indeed happened, marked *the* beginning—the original creation of all things. The scientist does not expect something to come from nothing. He has a dogged conviction that, if an explosion occured, something must have been there to explode. Does the universe run in an immense cycle, exploding, outrushing for eons into space — falling at last back in upon itself, congregating, concentrating, making of itself a vast nuclear bomb that repeats the process? Or does empty space give birth to matter, and matter return again to empty space? Or did the universe really arise from nothing four billion years ago? Nobody knows. But we grow bigger for wondering." 5

In this quotation, which is typical of those found in science books, we find a complete rejection of any belief in God. What Rush states nobody knows, scripture states in the first verse of the Bible. Rush deals in speculations based on human knowledge while scripture offers a simple statement which we accept by faith.

Let us see what George K. Schweitzer, a highly trained scientist who believes the Bible, has to say about opinions:

"However, we must never forget that all our scientific ideas relating to the ultimate questions of the universe come under the category of hypothesis. They are subject to constant revision." 6

17

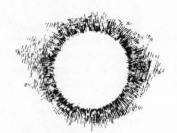

The history of science is a history of a succession of theories and hypotheses which were proposed and then replaced by some later idea. Since this is true, is it possible to harmonize scripture which is unchanging with theories which are changing?

Schweitzer further says:

"Attempts to avoid the idea of creation are found throughout the scientific literature, indicating the presence of much prejudice. Many writers are not content to leave the idea alone, which would be the strict scientific attitude since science does not deal with ultimate origins, but instead they take particular pains to set forth and promote belief in possibilities for a universe without an origin." 7

Not only do they attempt to explain away the Bible but they reveal an attitude of contempt for those who accept its teachings.

In conclusion Schweitzer says:

"Thus we may conclude that with reference to our positions as scientists we must not make a premature judgment on the mechanism of creation, but as children of the One True God we may affirm with the inspired author of the book of Hebrews that by faith we understand that the world was created by the word of God." 8

This is our conclusion, too.

SUGGESTED ACTIVITIES

1. What is the basic difference between the Biblical account of the creation and the scientific theories about the origin of the universe?

----

2. Explain why it is highly improbable that scientists ever will be able to explain how the universe started.

----

3. If God had explained how He created the universe, do you think we could have understood it? Explain:

---

4. Read the quotation from Rush on page 17. Explain how Rush refuses to recognize the Creator yet admits a doubt about the supposed natural origin of the universe.

---

5. Probably someone in the class can find an account of some other theory as to the origin of the earth and universe. If so, tell the class about the idea. Compare it with other theories.

6. Divide the class into two groups. Allow five minutes for each side to prepare its points for a debate on one of the following subjects:
   a. It is impossible to explain the origin of the universe without including God.
   b. The origin of the universe can be explained without a Creator.
   c. It is not necessary that we know how the universe came into being.

7. If one is available, visit a planetarium or observatory.

REFERENCES

1. Hurley, Patrick M., *How Old is the Earth?*, Doubleday and Company, Inc., Garden City, N. Y., 1959, p. 12.
2. Ibid., p. 152.
3. Rush, J. H., *The Dawn of Life*, New American Library of World Literature, Inc., New York, 1957, p. 41.
4. Ibid., p. 56.
5. Ibid., pp. 64-65.
6. Mixter, Russell L., (Editor), *Evolution and Christian Thought*, "The Origin of the Universe", by George K. Schweitzer, Wm. B. Eerdmans Publishing Company, Grand Rapids, 1959, p. 51.
7. Ibid., p. 51.
8. Ibid., p. 52.

LESSON 3

THE ORIGIN OF LIFE

Scripture: Gen. 1:11-13; 20-25 God created the living world for man to use.

Concerning origins, there are two big problems which biologists of today are studying: (1) the origin of life on earth and (2) the possibility of creating life in the laboratory. In this lesson we shall examine the Biblical account of the creation of life, the leading scientific theories as to how life originated, the efforts to produce life in the laboratory, and some of the arguments against the scientific theories.

The Biblical Account

In Genesis 1 we have the account of God's creation of living organisms. We find there that God prepared the earth first and then placed plants on the globe. The plants are merely classified as grasses, herbs, and trees. These are the seed bearing plants. No mention is made of fungi, algae, mosses, and ferns along with their relatives. These plants may have been included in the herbs or the grasses. Many extinct plants were not mentioned in this account. On the fifth day only two kinds of animals were created, aquatic animals and flying creatures. It is specified that "every living creature" in the water was created. This includes shellfish, worms, corals, jellyfish, and innumerable other water animals. "Every winged fowl after his kind" implies bats and

insects as well as birds On the sixth day land animals were created. This includes worms, reptiles, amphibians, mammals, and hosts of others. Then as the grand finale God said, "Let us make man in our image . . . " So man, a spiritual being, created in the image of God, appeared.

In these few verses is recorded the creation of all life. From them we learn that God created all life and that it was good. The implication is of a complete, perfect creation.

God's command to multiply implies adult forms ready to reproduce.

Scientific Theory of the Origin of Life

As in the case of the origin of the universe scientists completely omit God in their theories. Note this quotation from Rush:

"Today, of course, the belief that living things were especially created for an earth prepared to receive them finds no scientific support. The earlier view of cosmos as a fixed,

unalterable product of special creation has given way to the understanding that the very seas and mountains change and evolve with the passing of the ages. From a scientific standpoint, life must be regarded also as an aspect of nature that evolves with the environment." 1

Before coming to present theories of how life originated we will note two abandoned ideas. The first is called *Spontaneous Generation.* Throughout the middle ages people commonly held to the idea that living things often arose from non-living substances. F o r example frogs were thought to arise from mud or slime in a pond and maggots from decaying meat. Worms, insects, and many other creatures were thought to be formed by the materials in which they lived.

An Italian named Redi, in 1668 questioned meat as the source of maggots. He performed some experiments in which he proved that decaying meat would not get maggots unless flies could contact it. Few paid any attention to this experiment and even Redi himself failed to see the application to other situations.

With the discovery of the use of the microscope by the Dutchman Leeuwenhoek, scientists were able to see tiny organisms in water. A pupil of Leeuwenhoek's, Jablot, proved that broth boiled and kept sealed would not acquire such life but that which was boiled and left exposed to the air soon had an abundance of living things in it.

Others did some experimenting but it was the Frenchman, Pasteur, who really clenched the matter. He, too, used nutrient solutions but he used cotton plugs in the flasks to filter out the bacteria as the air entered the flask containing the sterile broth. Those flasks containing sterile broth did not become contaminated.

Following these experiments the theory of spontaneous generation was replaced by the belief in biogenesis. Today biologists believe that life comes from preexisting life. Stated simply: all living things have parents. However, we find the evolutionists leave one important exception to this law. They do not accept the creation recorded in the Bible. If life did not come from God, then it had to come from nonliving substances at some time. So, they violate their own belief.

Life in the Universe

With spontaneous generation proven impossible and with an aversion to accepting special creation according to the Bible, people searched for another explanation of the origin of life. Accordingly the theory of "cosmozoa" arose. "Cosmo"—universe plus "zoa"—animals means living things in the universe. Some thought living bits of matter may have come to earth on meteorites. Soon it was realized life could not exist on terrifically hot meteorites. The Swede, Arrhenius, proposed other ways in which he thought life may have arrived on earth from somewhere in the universe. It is known now that ultraviolet light would kill any such life. Also, this theory fails to explain the origin of the first life.

Chemical Origin

The Russian, A. I. Oparin, published his theory as to how life originated, the English translation of which was first copyrighted in 1938. Oparin's proposals explained in his book, *Origin of Life*, form the basis of the commonly held theory of today. Scientists vary in their ideas as to details but the basic points are virtually the same. No effort will be made in this work to explain the complex chemical changes proposed by Oparin or others but only the general high points will be presented.

1. The earth once was much like the sun, being extremely hot and composed of the same chemicals.

2. Through eons of time the earth cooled and seas formed of complex chemicals appeared.

3. Some chemicals formed gummy masses called coacervates. Coacervates are small masses of molecules held together in larger masses by a thin layer of water. (Coacervates are not theoretical masses but the idea of their forming in primeval seas is theoretical.)

4. Some coacervates were unstable and broken apart while others held together.

5. The coacervates used other chemicals in the water as "food" when they grew. Also, they gave off waste. This exchange took place through the film of water.

6. Eventually some of the coacervates became able to split in two and grow into two masses (reproduction).

7. The coacervates increased in numbers and used up the surrounding chemicals until a shortage of food developed.

8. Then some of the coacervates learned to manufacture their own food.

9. The coacervates which could not make food ate or used those which could make food as food for themselves.

10. Then some bodies acquired chlorophyll and began manufacturing sugar and giving off oxygen. They were the first plants.

11. Those not able to manufacture food ate the green masses and so were the first animals. Life had appeared on the earth.

12. These primitive plants and animals then changed form through the ages until present day organisms including man evolved.

By using dating techniques discussed in a later lesson scientists estimate the age of the earth to be about 4.5 billion years. The date of the first apparance of green plants, algae, is set at 2 billion years ago. Therefore they assign some 2 billion years as the time required for the chemical changes or evolution which produced life to take place.

The first changes are supposed to have taken place by chance. The more stable (fittest) compounds lasted while others broke down. So this was a continuation of the evolution that started with the formation of the stars and planets themselves. Chance changes with the best adapted surviving continued to occur until man appeared as the climax.

We have noted that spontaneous generation, or the idea that living things of today come from nonliving material, has been proven untrue and is rejected by scientists. Adler states the law of biogenesis this way:

"It is a law of life that living things come only from living things, and like produces like." 2

Yet evolutionary scientists believe that life in the beginning formed from nonliving substances. One might ask why that process is not accepted today. Laboratory experiments and observation prove beyond question that all living things have parents and that they are like their parents. Evolutionists explain the discrepancy in this way. They say there was no oxygen in the atmosphere in the beginning and the chemical composition of the water was different. The layer of ozone (a form of oxygen) now in the air filters out the ultra-violet rays of the sun which they think may have provided the energy involved in the early chemical changes. Ultra-violet light at full strength kills life. How could it provide energy to create life? If any living structure should evolve from non-living material today they would immediately be destroyed by the living things already present, they say. That being true, life could not originate now as they believe it did in the past. In short, present conditions are so different life could not rise by evolution again. In this way evolutionists get around a difficulty.

To assume that atmospheric conditions at the beginning of life were different from the conditions of today is to contradict the doctrine of uniformitarianism. Uniformitarianism assumes that conditions on the earth have always been the same or that natural processes have not changed. The Biblical doctrine, catastrophism, accepts the flood of Noah which was a catastrophe which interrupted the natural processes. Evolutionists believe the natural processes have not changed, but they have to assume different conditions at the beginning if life arose spontaneously.

Creating Life

Strange to say, even though scientists do not believe in spontaneous generation today, they have an idea of being able to create life in the laboratory, and extensive research is being done in that field. Some scientists confidently believe it is only a matter of time until life is created by man. For many years scientists assumed man could not manufacture substances produced by living processes. However, Wohler produced urea in the laboratory in 1828. That started a long line of research. Then in 1953 Stanley Miller and Harold Urey produced some amino acids. These substances are the units which make up proteins while proteins are the chief materials comprising living cells. Sydney Fox has done additional research. Not only has he failed to produce protein but he frankly recognizes the tremendous odds to be met.

Protein molecules are so extremely complex that scientists do not know the structure of many of them though much has been learned about the structure of cells. The Frenchman, Lecomte du Nouy, estimated that it would take 10^{243} (10 followed by 243 zeros) billions of years for one molecule of protein to form on the earth by chance according to the leading theory concerning the origin of life. 3 If it takes that long for one molecule to form, how long would it take for a cell made of molecules to form? When one considers this one sees the high improbability of such a thing happening in the distant past on earth or in the laboratory.

Even if proteins could be formed by natural means there still would be the problem of life itself. Scientists have never been able to define life. They can only tell the differences between living and non-living things. Some evolutionists of today define life as merely being a state of complexity. That is, when molecules assumed a very complex arrangement they then were alive. No effort is made to describe the degree of complexity or its nature. An indefinable "something" enables living things to use oxygen, digest and use food, move, reproduce, grow, and respond to stimuli. Could a scientist instill these abilities into a protein molecule if he should ever make such a structure?

When one considers all these problems it becomes much easier and simpler just to accept what God said. Scientists recognize that all life comes from pre-existing life. If that is true today and scientists recognize that there had to be a beginning, then that beginning had to originate outside the universe. That leaves God, the Eternal One, as the source of all life on the earth. Only He can create life.

Conclusion

We find God gives us a very simple statement of His creation of both non-living and living things. Evolutionists reject that statement and believe life just started by chance in some ancient ocean. This is contradictory to the law of biogenesis: Life comes from pre-existing life, and young always resemble their parents. This law has been verified by experimentation and by observation. Scientists expect to be able to create life in the laboratory. The extreme complexity of protein makes the chemical process highly unlikely. Then since life comes from pre-existing life, it is reasonable to believe only God has produced life or can produce life.

SUGGESTED ACTIVITIES

1. If life should be discovered on other planets, would that affect the truth of the Bible? Explain your answer.

----

2. Explain the discrepancy between the Law of Biogenesis and Oparin's theory as to the origin of life.

----

3. Since God is the source of life, do you think man will ever be able to create life? ---

4. Why is it of importance that Christians know about these theories? ---

----

----

5. Let different members of the class make reports on these subjects:
   a. The Stanley Miller Experiment
   b. The Sydney Fox Experiment
   (Note: These experiments are described in recent biology texts as well as in library books.)

6. During the Middle Ages people believed God created the earth and living things. They also believed in spontaneous generation. How were they inconsistent?

----

7. Find articles in recent publications describing the efforts now being made to find out whether or not there is life in outer space. Discuss the relation of the articles to scripture. Add such clippings to the scrap book or bulletin board.

REFERENCES

1. Rush, Joseph Harold, *The Dawn of Life*, copyright 1957 by Joseph Harold Rush, p. 96.
2. Adler, Irving, *How Life Began*, The John Day Company, Inc., New York, 1957, p. 15.
3. du Nouy, Lecomte, *Human Destiny*, Longmans, Green and Company, New York, 1947, p. 34.

LESSON 4

THE ORIGIN OF MAN

Scripture: Gen. 1:26-27; Gen. 2:7; Acts. 17:24-28 God gave us both physical and spiritual life.

"And God said, Let us make man in our image . . . And God created man in his own image. — And Jehovah God caused a deep sleep to fall upon the man, and he slept; and he took one of his ribs and closed up the flesh instead thereof: and the rib, which Jehovah God had taken from man, made he a woman, and brought her unto the man." Gen. 1, 2; Gen. 1:26; 2:21-22.

In a few simple words God tells us that we are made in His image; that he created us according to His plan. As Christians we believe this simple account. But almost certainly prehistoric man as seen in the comics, text books, and many other places make part of your thinking about man. In this lesson we shall examine the basis for such ideas of man and relate them to the Bible.

The Fossils on Which Prehistoric Man is Based

What is the basis of the pictures of prehistoric man with his stooped posture, shaggy hair, and coarse features? Is it scientifically accurate? If so, how do we relate it to the Genesis account? Let us first consider the most important fossils found to this date.

G. W. Lasker provides a simple classification of human or near human fossils. He classifies them as "(1) manlike apes, (2) apelike men, (3) primitive species of man, and (4) fossil types of man, members of our species, Homo sapiens." 1

Beginning farther back in so-called evolutionary history it is believed fishes evolved from simpler animals. Some fishes became amphibians, some amphibians became reptiles, and some reptiles became mammals. One branch of the mammals became primates. The primates include such animals as monkeys, baboons, and apes and also man.

The Primate line is made up of the mammals leading up to man. The simplest or presumably the earliest types are called

28

Prosimians (before the simians). They include animals such as lemurs, lorises, and tree shrews. The monkeys branched off from the Prosimians early and the Pongidae formed a branch which includes apes, baboons, and gorillas. Then the Hominidae or human beings appeared as the most advanced branch.

Among the fossil Pongidae are a number of forms found in Africa which might be termed man-apes. There are a variety of them. Most of the fossils are only fragments and anthropologists disagree in many instances about their significance. Among the most famous of these fossils is Proconsul discovered by Mrs. L. S. B. Leakey in Tanganyika, Africa. All of these fossils are regarded as entirely animal by anthropologists even though some of them possess some hominid (human) characteristics.

A rather diverse group of fossils found in Africa are called the Australopithecinae (southern apes). They were found in limestone formations in quarries or caves. Professor Raymond Dart and Dr. Robert Broom found and named most of the fossils. Two were called Australopithecus, two Paranthropus, and one Plesianthropus. They show many similarities and were grouped into the Australopithecinae.

The first specimen of Australopithecus was discovered in 1924 with others following in the next few years. Then in 1959 Mrs. Leakey discovered in Africa the skull of a creature which Dr. Leakey named Zinjanthropus. The skull was chipped out of solid rock and was in about four hundred pieces. Thus it is hard to estimate its size and shape. This fossil became the basis of "Zinj", the well-known character with enormous face and small brain (not Neanderthal Man) seen in recent science books. The jaw was not found with this fossil, so the huge jaw in the restoration was the product of the imagination of the one drawing the picture. In 1964 Richard Leakey, son of Dr. Leakey, discovered a jaw which was assumed to be that of another specimen of Zinjanthropus. The two finds were sixty-five miles apart. As a result of the second find very different pictures of "Zinj" now are appearing with the jaw much reduced in size. This serves to illustrate the high degree of uncertainty attached to the restorations commonly seen. Although these fossils were given different names by their discoverers, most leading anthropologists consider them all one group and call them the Australopithecinae.

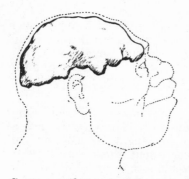

These fossils are very fragmentary and there are disagreements as to their age. In general they were creatures with a man-like pelvis indicating upright posture and bipedal locomotion. The jaws were large with teeth like man's. This is an important point. The brain is thought to have been small like the apes, but it should be remembered that the fossils were often broken and crushed. Some anthropologists consider these controversial creatures man-like apes and some regard them as ape-like men. Some evolutionists say they possibly were ancestors of modern man, while others say they were a branch which became extinct and therefore were not man's predecessors.

It should be remembered that evolutionists are searching for "proof" for their theory. Since they believe man descended from animals it is easy for them to regard any apparently unusual fossil as very old and probably a link between man and animals. Then they use their interpretations as evidence for evolution. Frequently they change their minds. For example, Dr. Leakey no longer considers Zinjanthropus as man's ancestor but now assigns that honor to Homo habilis, another fossil found in Africa. 2

A group of fossils found in parts of Java and China have been named Pithecanthropus (Apeman). They include Java Man and Peking Man. They were characterized by small brain capacity (between Homo and Australopithecus), large ridges over the eyes, a ridge on the top of the skull, large jaws, no chin, and large teeth. Although they differed in many respects they were considered to have been true humans. Peking Man used fire and made tools. No animal ever has done that. Mayr considers Pithecanthropus merely a form of Homo. 3 Dobzhansky expresses a similar opinion. 4

Fossils of Homo, or modern man fall into three major classifications. Neanderthal man was once considered a primitive form which evolved into Homo sapiens. He is the prehistoric man with bent posture, long hair, and heavy features seen in comic books and many other books. He is the so-called Cave Man. It is thought now that these people disappeared some time in the past and were not forerunners of Recent Man. From Lasker we learn some authorities believe the first discovered skeleton, on which the pictures are based, was an individual who had arthritis. He, as well as Dobzhansky and Mayr, considered Neanderthal Man to have been erect, not stooped in posture. 5, 6, 7. Many evolutionists of today consider

Neanderthal Man only a variation of modern man or Homo sapiens. Mayr leaves the classification of Neanderthal Man open but definitely states the form was not primitive. 8 The variations in Neanderthal Man such as sloping skull and large jaws and teeth are not so great that they can not be observed today. The skull capacity was fully as large as Recent Man's and the associated tools and other artifacts also indicate intelligence as high as that of Modern Man.

The status of Cro-Magnon Man, the second type, has never been questioned. This fine type was modern in every respect. The variations found are no greater than those seen in present day man. However the fossils indicate strong muscular individuals with brains larger than those of Modern Man. Cro-Magnon Man used tools and is believed to have produced the fine art work found in caves in southern Europe.

Anthropologists are puzzled as to what became of Neanderthal Man. Some believe Cro-Magnon Man conquered and drove him to extinction while others suggest the two types hybridized and the Neanderthalian traits became obliterated. Neither is there any explanation of Cro-Magnon Man; where he originated or why he disappeared. Also there are varying opinions as to whether either or both of these forms were ancestral to Recent Man or Homo sapiens, the third type.

Summary of Fossil Forms

In this brief discussion primate fossils have been placed in three major categories. First are found the large number of fossils that are considered unmistakably animal. Second, the group of African fossils referred to as Australopithecus, are considered by some to be low type humans. Their skeletons are quite human, but the skulls indicate possible low brain development. The teeth are human. Some consider Australopithecus an offshoot which was not in the line of human evolution. The third classification is considered purely human. It includes two sub-divisions, Pithecanthropus and Homo. Dobzhansky classifies Pithecanthropus and Homo as one genus calling both Homo. 9   Thus we see the only group of fossils which could be considered a transition between animal and human forms is the Australopithecines and· they were far more human than animal.

Some Difficulties in Human Paleontology

Human paleontology presents many difficulties to the anthropologist. First there is the great scarcity of such fossils and their fragmentary character. 10   Dating presents a major problem. In addition to being dated by the same methods as are other fossils, human fossils are partly dated by the artifacts found with them. Still another problem is presented by the fact that parts of a skeleton may be scattered so it can't be certain that all the bones in one locality belong to the same individual. The fact that fossils consist only of bones is still another difficulty. Hair, skin, and internal organs aren't preserved. Often there is a question as to whether the fragments of bones are human or animal or which sex they may be. Age of the individual at the time of death is another problem.

The pictures one sees of prehistoric forms are based on very scant remains in some cases and are subject to great error. The varying opinions of anthropologists about human fossils indicated how much uncertainty is attached to many of them.

The Missing Links

The missing links, and there are many, occur at crucial points. The ancestors of the various major classifications are missing. That is true, too, in the case of man's supposed evolution from an ape-like ancestry. Let us note some quotations from leading scientists:'

"There is a long gap in the fossil record between the early Miocene of eastern Africa, with its rich deposits of anthropoids, and the early Pleistocene, again rich in hominid fossils." . . . .

"It is consequently not known through what stages the hominid line went in the Miocene and Pliocene." 11

"There is not merely one 'missing link' but a whole series of grades of 'missing links' in hominid history." 12

"The fact is that the most serious hiatus now in the hominid evolution is the gap which separates the genus Australopithecus from the fossil hominids of Pliocene and Miocene times" . . . .

"So far no fossil remains of undoubted hominids have been found in geological deposits which can with any certainty be assigned to an antiquity greater than early Pleistocene . . . Pliocene hominids have been postulated and it is certain that they existed, but their relics have yet to be discovered . . ." 13

"Since evolution is a continuous process we would not find gaps anywhere, if we could know all the links between the common ancestor and the now living species; cutting the continuum into species or races would then be arbitrary. The incompleteness of the fossil record here, strange to say, a help— the 'missing links' are convenient breaks which are used to draw race or species boundaries." 14

From these quotations we see there is no known link between man and animals so far as the fossil evidence is concerned. And the fossils are considered by evolutionists to be the evidence of the evolution that has taken place. There is a big gap between animal fossils and the Australopithecines.

Variations in Human Types

It is not a matter of concern that the fossils often show variations from present day man. One only has to observe the many kinds of dogs to realize how much one species can vary in size, proportions, color, and type of hair. Is there any reason why man can not vary, too? Most of the most obvious characteristics of fossil men can be seen today. Some have large jaws as did Neanderthal Man and a sloping forehead is not unknown. Heavy bones and ridges over the eyes can be found. Size and body builds are quite variable, too. Size and shape of the skull, except in the case of some abnormalities, has nothing to do with the level of intelligence. A man five feet tall will have a smaller skull than a man six feet tall because the body is proportioned. Intelligence is not determined by body size. So it is entirely possible or probable that the Australopithecines were true people. The body skeleton is quite human.

If man's appearance h a s changed some since God put him here it would not be surprising. Domesticated animals have changed. But the changes are merely variations within a species. That is not evolution. The races are variations within t h e species. Scripture does not explain races and science can only theorize.

Special Problems of Human Evolution

Man is more than an animal. He has a soul. If man evolved slowly from animal ancestors, when did he become human and when did God deal with him as a man? How can evolution from an animal be harmonized with the account of man's fall in the garden? How can Adam and Eve as individuals be accounted for if people evolved?

Conclusions

Human fossils are few in number compared to many other species and they are often very fragmentary. The Australopithecines are the only fossils which are even remotely questionable and they can be low type humans. Pithecanthropus is true man and is called Homo by some paleontologists. There are three major types of Homo: Neanderthal Man, Cro-Magon Man, and Recent Man. The variations in these types are no more than might be found today. The animal fossils are unmistakably animal. Since these facts are true we find no reason to feel the fossil evidence contradicts the Bible.

SUGGESTED ACTIVITIES

1. What do evolutionists omit in their descriptions of man?

2. What characteristics of man did God refer to when He said, " . . . make man in our image"?

3. Can one believe in the evolution of lower animals and reject the evolution of man? Discuss.

4. Describe the three basic types of fossil people.

   a.

   b.

   c.

5. Different human types are mentioned in the Bible. Read the following references and describe the person or persons.

a. Gen. 27:11 _____

_____

b. Num. 13:32 _____

c. I. Sam. 10:23_____

d. I. Sam. 16:12_____

e. Lk. 19:2-4 _____

6. Obtain some bones from an animal or bird. Crush them and demonstrate the difficulty of fitting them together. Relate this to the skull of "Zinje."

7. Evolutionists emphasize the ways fossil humans supposedly were different from modern man. Actually the types can be found today. Study the heads of people you meet at school or church. Look for sloping foreheads, bony ridges where the eyebrows are, and receding chins.

REFERENCES

1. Lasker, G. W., *The Evolution of Man*, Holt, Rinehart and Winston, Inc., New York, 1961, p. 91.

2. Payne, Melvin M., "Family in Search of Prehistoric Man," *National Geographic*, vol. 127, No. 2, February, 1965, pp. 194-231.

3. Mayr, Ernst, *Animal Species and Evolution*, Harvard University Press, Cambridge, 1963, p. 632.

4. Dobzhansky, Theodosius, *Mankind Evolving*, Yale University Press, New Haven, Connecticut, 1962, p. 176.

5. Lasker, op. cit., p. 104, 105.

6. Dobzhansky, op. cit., p. 332.

7. Mayr, op. cit., p. 641

8. Ibid., p. 642.

9. Dobzhansky, op. cit., p. 186.

10. Clark, Le Gros, *The Fossil Evidence for Human Evolution*, University of Chicago Press, Chicago, 1955, p. 46.

11. Mayr, op. cit., p. 628.

12. Ibid., 637.

13. Clark, op. cit., p. 163.

14. Dobzhansky, op. cit., p. 186.

"IN THE BEGINNING GOD..."

LESSON 5

DATES AND TIME

Scripture: Gen. 1:1-31; Job 38:1-7 Like Job of old we were not present at the creation but through faith we accept the account of that event as God revealed it to us.

How old is the earth? When did life originate? Much has been written and many studies have been made about these two questions. What does the Bible teach about these problems? Do the discoveries and theories of the scientists prove the Bible false? These questions are of great importance to Christians. We will study some phases of these problems in this lesson.

In Genesis 1:1-10; 14-19 we have the Biblical account of the origin of the earth as a place suitable for living things. The student should study those passages carefully before continuing with this lesson.

In the Beginning

The first three words in the Bible tell us all we know about when the earth and the rest of the universe were created. *In the beginning* just means the beginning of time. Scripture gives no date in terms of years. The date 4004 B. C. is found in the marginal notes of many King James Bibles. It was first placed in the King James Bible in 1701 and never has been part of the text. Archbishop Ussher, an Anglican priest, arrived at this date by adding the lengths of the lives of the patriarchs as given in Genesis 5 and 11. In Genesis 5 is a chronology of the patriarchs from Adam to Noah's sons. In Genesis 11 the chronology is extended from Shem to Abraham. Old Testament dates from the time of Abraham on are fairly accurate. In many instances scripture gives the number of years between events. Besides, archeologists have ways of correlating Biblical history and profane history and thus establishing dates. The accepted date of 1921 B.C. ascribed to Abraham probably is close to correct. Ussher totaled the years of the pre-Abrahamic patriarchs and added the total to the date of Abraham and arrived at 4004 B. C. as the date of Adam.

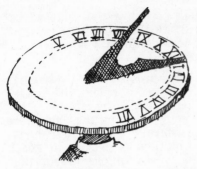

There are three questionable aspects of this method of determining the date of creation. First, the list of patriarchs named may not be complete, and second, the ages of the fathers are questionable. By comparing the different chronologies in the Bible it seems evident that they were not meant to be complete lists of all the ancestors of certain individuals but merely indicate line of descent. In such cases the term "son" means "descendent of" instead of son as we use the term today. In Matt. 1:11 we have these words, "and Josias begat Jechonias—" But from II Kings 22:1; 23-34; and 24:6 we learn that Jechonias (Jehoiachin) was the grandson of Josias (Josiah). Matthew uses the term "son" as we use the word "descendant." Other examples could be given but this is enough to illustrate the uncertainty that all the men in the line of descent of Abraham are named.

The second uncertainty in Ussher's date is the question concerning the ages of the patriarchs. The Old Testament was written largely in Hebrew. About three hundred years before Christ a Greek translation called the Septuagint was made. In making the translations and copies errors sometimes occur. The Septuagint and the ancient Hebrew texts do not always agree as to the ages of the patriarchs. (It should be noted that the points of disagreement are not such as would affect the basic principles of how to become a Christian and live the Christian life.) By using the figures in the Septuagint the date 5556 B.C. is arrived at as the date of Adam as contrasted with Ussher's 4004 B.C. derived from the Hebrew texts.

The third problem is the uncertainty as to how much the lives of the patriarchs overlapped. Scripture does not make that clear.

Origin of Matter and Life: Dates

The date 4004 B.C. is commonly thought of as the Biblical date of the creation of the entire universe. Not only is the date questionable as the date of Adam but how much time elapsed between the original creation of the matter of the universe and the creation of Adam is subject to question. In Genesis 1:1 we are told that God created the heavens and the earth "in the beginning." Following that statement is a description of the chaotic condition of the earth. No hint is given as to when "in the beginning" was in terms of years nor how long the chaotic state lasted. The belief that a long period of time elapsed between Genesis 1:1 and Genesis 1:2 is called the "gap theory." This theory will be discussed in more detail in a later lesson.

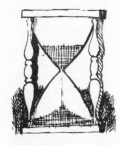

Still another problem relative to early dates is the problem of how long the "days" of Genesis 1 were. Until the advent of extensive evolutionary teaching the days were assumed to be literally twenty-four hours long. When evolutionists began to teach that organisms slowly changed form they had to assume immense periods of time because obviously if changes took place they were very slow. Under the attacks of evolutionists, theologians began trying to "harmonize" science and scripture. If God created by evolutionary processes as some believed then there had to be long periods of time and the theory arose that the "days" were geological ages billions of years long.

There are several arguments in favor of twenty-four hour days. Linguists tell us the Hebrew word, "yom", translated "day" is used in a number of ways. Sometimes it means the light part of the day, sometimes as the entire twenty-four hours, and at times a period of time or a future date is meant. Note what Surburg says:

"In evaluating these various interpretations bear in mind that *yom* occurs no fewer than 1,480 times in the Old Testament and that it is properly translated by over 50 different words, including 'time', 'life', 'to-day', 'age', 'forever', 'continually', and 'perpetually'." 1

The meaning of the word is indicated by the context. Linguists tell us the word means twenty-four hours when it is preceded by a definite numeral such as the "first" day or the "second" day. That is the case in Genesis. A second argument is the use of the phrase, "evening and morning" implying days as we know them.

From Genesis there is only one argument in favor of long periods of time. The sun, moon, and stars were set as means of measuring time on the fourth day. Since they did not measure the first three days, then the term "day" might mean periods of time as it obviously does in some scriptures. There are other theories as to the meaning of the "days" of Genesis which will not be discussed in this work.

By way of summary it might be said that from scripture it is impossible to set a date for creation for the following reasons:

1. Original creation was "in the beginning" which gives no hint in terms of years.

2. The length of time from original creation of matter to Adam can't be determined because we don't know how long the period of chaos was, how long the "days" were, or whether there was a gap between original creation and a second creation in which life was formed. (To be discussed in more detail later.)

3. The date of Adam's creation can't be determined.

It isn't necessary that we accept any one of the theories or explanations in order to believe the Bible. God told us He created the heavens and the earth with all the living things on the earth. That is enough for the Christian.

Scientific Methods of Dating the Universe

Having considered Biblical evidence, or more accurately lack of evidence, as to the age of the earth, we will now examine briefly some of the scientific methods of establishing dates. First it should be explained that the scientist deals with two kinds of time, absolute time and relative time. Absolute time is the time in terms of years since events took place. For example if we say the earth is 4.5 billion years old we are dealing with absolute time. Relative time refers to dates as compared with other dates. The scientist may say the Cretaceous Age is younger than the Pennsylvania Age or the Quaternary is younger than the Jurassic. Scientists attempt to arrive at absolute age by finding ways of determining numbers of years while they determine relative time by fossil sequence. The fossil sequence is determined by supposed order of evolution. If the fossils in one stratum (layer) of rock supposedly evolved earlier than those of another stratum, then the relative age is older.

Methods of Determining Absolute Age

A number of methods of estimating the age of the earth have been used. One of the first used rate of erosion as a basis. However, scientists discovered that rate of erosion is variable so that method of estimation was abandoned. Some tried to use the rate of accumulation of salt in the ocean but that, too, was found to be undependable. Other methods were proposed and discarded.

The method commonly used today is based on the decay rate of certain elements. Uranium, thorium, potassium, and rubidium are used. We will base this discussion on uranium since it is most commonly used. Uranium slowly breaks down into lead and helium. The helium is a gas and escapes. A piece of rock containing uranium will also contain lead produced by the breakdown of uranium. Thorium also breaks down into lead and helium and is found associated with uranium. Some lead, called nonradiogenic, is not formed by decay of uranium or thorium but is assumed always to have been lead. The rate of conversion of uranium and thorium to lead is known. There is no known variation in conditions such as temperature which will alter the rate of decay. By determining the percentage of each of the elements in a piece of rock, scientists estimate how long the decay process has been in progress and from this the age of the earth. To use this method of determining dates five conditions must be assumed to be true. They are as follows:

"The 'ore method' assumes (1) that the rocks contained only uranium, thorium, and nonradiogenic lead (lead which is not the product of radioactive decay) at the time the earth's crust was formed; (2) that changes in the ratio of uranium and lead or thorium and lead have not occurred since the time the earth's crust was formed except for radioactive decay; (3) that each lead ore has been derived from a single area and has not been mixed with lead from another source; (4) that we can determine the amounts of uranium, thorium, and non radiogenic lead originally present; (5) and that the rate of decay which is constant today and can be neither speeded up nor slowed down, has been constant since the origin of the rocks." 2

A close look at these five conditions will reveal the fact that they can't be proven. (1) God could have created the rocks with any proportion of the elements. There is no way to prove the composition of the rocks at the origin of the earth's crust. (2) There is no way to know what changes other than decay may have taken place in the remote past. (3) There is evidence of considerable mixing of some rocks. (4) There is no way to measure the amounts of these elements originally present. (5) although rate of decay, so far as scientists have been able to determine, is unchangeable today, there is no way to prove that always has been the case.

Still another weakness in this method lies in the very few kinds of rocks that can be used for such dating. There are further weaknesses recognized by scientists which will not be discussed here.

A less widely used method of estimating the age of the earth is called the "Meteorite Method." By this plan the lead composition of the earth and meteorites is compared. It is assumed that the composition of the earth and meteorites was the same at the time of origin. In the earth's surface radioactive decay has taken place. So by comparing the kinds of lead of the earth with the kinds found in meteorites scientists arrived at 4.5 billion years as the age of the earth. Again assumptions which can't be proven are present. There is no way to prove that meteorites and the earth were of the same composition at the beginning nor can be determined the changes that may or may not have taken place in either the earth or meteorites.

Dating Fossil Remains

Evolutionists are very much concerned with the ages of fossils. They have determined what they think are the relative ages of various fossils (this will be discussed in another lesson) but they would like to confirm this with proven absolute ages. This is considered of great importance in the study of human fossils. Two main methods are used to estimate the ages of fossils.

By the fluoride method the scientist assumes bones to have contained little or no fluorine at the death of the animal. After the bones were buried they absorbed fluorine from the water. By determining the amount of fluorine in a fossil bone the scientist tries to estimate its age. Again there are weaknesses. Human beings drink water from different sources. The fluorine content of different waters is highly variable resulting in different amounts being absorbed by bones of the same age.

The Carbon 14, or as it is written the C^{14}, method is considered reasonably accurate for dates as far back as 25,000 years. Some hope newer techniques now in the experimental stage may enable scientists to push back the dates to about 44,000 years. All living things contain carbon which is derived from the carbon dioxide in the air. Most of the carbon is called C^{12} and is not radioactive. Radioactive carbon, C^{14}, is present in very small but known percentage. After an organism dies no further acquisition of carbon takes place and the

41

$C14$ slowly breaks down to $C12$. By estimating the amount of $C14$ present and comparing that to the known rate of decay the scientist arrives at an absolute age, or age in terms of years, of the fossil.

This method also is subject to sources of inaccuracy similar to those of other methods of dating, but scientists have had some way of confirming accuracy. Klotz has this to say:

"Where it has been possible to correlate these dates with known historical dates, radiocarbon dating appears to be fairly reliable. A number of tests have been made, and these have agreed rather closely with known historical dates." 3

The reasonable accuracy of radiocarbon dating has had some interesting effects on the battle between the evolution-ist's long periods of time as well at the six thousand years so often accepted by Christians. Ages of fossils indicate life has been here a few thousand years longer than six thousand but not nearly as long as evolutionists supposed.

Conclusions

From this lesson it can be concluded that Christians need not be concerned by the apparent discrepancy between Biblical dates and scientific dates. In the first place scripture gives no date for either the creation of the materials of the universe or for the creation of living things. The commonly held 4004 B.C. has no reliable scriptural basis. Likewise all methods used by man to date either the rocks of the earth or fossil remains are subject to error. Since these facts are true then there is no true discrepancy between scientific estimates of dates and theological (not Biblical) estimates. It is impor-tant that we believe that God did create both the universe and life, not that we know when or how such creation took place.

SUGGESTED ACTIVITIES

1. Explain why the problem of time is so important in the conflict between evolution and the Bible.

----

2. Explain why we do not have to be concerned about the time of creation.

_____

_____

_____

_____

3. Explain how a faulty method of studying the Bible has contributed to much misunderstanding on the part of both scientists and theologians.

_____

_____

_____

_____

_____

_____

4. Dr. Leakey estimated the age of Zinjanthropus to be about 1,750,000 years. However, the bones themselves were not dated but the rocks in which the bones were found were dated. Explain why the assumption that the bones are the same age as the rocks is not reliable.

_____

_____

_____

_____

_____

5. Be sure to keep the collection of newspaper and magazine articles up to date. Discuss any articles found dealing with dates or the age of the earth or of man.

REFERENCES

1. Zimmerman, Paul A. (Editor), *Darwin, Evolution and Creation*, "In the Beginning God Created", by Raymond F. Surburg, Concordia Publishing House, St. Louis, Missouri, 1959, p. 58.
2. Klotz, John W., *Genes, Genesis, and Evolution*, Concordia Publishing House, St. Louis, Missouri, 1955, p. 102.
3. Ibid., p. 112.

LESSON 6
CLASSIFICATION AND THE EVOLUTIONARY TREE

Scripture: Gen. 2:16-17; Gen. 3:1-8; Rev. 22:1-2   The Bible begins with a tree in a garden and closes with a tree in heaven; both trees very different from the evolutionary tree of life.

For many years man has attempted to organize the vast number of living things into some kind of classification scheme. The first attempts were often crude since people knew so little about plant or animal structure.   The great Swedish scientist, Linnaeus, devised the system called the binomial system which is the basis of the present day method of classification.   This system was accepted by scientists about two hundred years ago. In this lesson we will examine the Linnean system of classification and relate it to both the Bible and the theory of evolution.

The Linnean System of Classification

According to Linnaeus' scheme all organisms were divided into two kingdoms—plant and animal.   In very recent years a third kingdom, the protista, has been accepted by some scientists.   The protista are simple organisms which are like animals in some ways and like plants in some respects.   Authorities are not in agreement as to which organisms should be included in the protista.   However, most organisms can be called definitely plant or animal.   The kingdoms are then classified into major divisions called *phyla* (sing. phylum).   Each phylum is further subdivided into *subphyla* which in turn are divided into *classes*.   Classes are grouped into *orders* and orders into *families*.   *Genera* make up the families and the subdivisions of genera are called *species*.   According to this scheme let us see how a dog is classified.

CLASSIFICATION OF THE DOG

Kingdom—Animal.

Phylum—Chordata (All have a cartilagonous cord in the back at least during embryonic development).

Subphylum—Vertebrata (All have a spinal column composed of vertebrae).

Class—Mammalia (Animals that have hair on their bodies and suckle their young).

Order—Carnivora (Meat-eating animals).

Family—Canidae (Dogs, wolves, jackals and foxes).

Genus—Canis (Dogs, wolves, jackals).

Species—familiaris (Dogs).

Scientists call the dog *Canis familiaris*. There are two parts to the name, the genus name (always written with a capital letter) and the species name (written with a small letter). That is why the name is said to be binomial.

The Evolutionary Tree

Linnaeus did not believe in evolution but believed that God created all living things in the same form that he saw. He classified organisms according to their structure. Evolutionists have taken the same scheme and used it to show supposed evolutionary relationships. They say organisms with similar structure have a common ancestor and are closely related while organisms with less similar structures are less closely related and their common ancestor is more remote. Let us

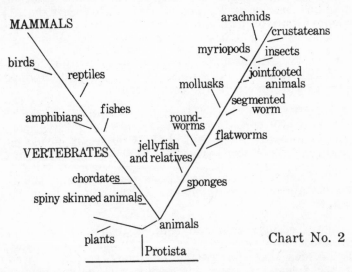

Chart No. 2

study the much simplified evolutionary "tree" on Chart No. 2. We remember from a previous lesson that evolutionists believe that life originated as simple structures in the ocean. Some became plants and some became animals and started those two kingdoms. Some remained neither definitely plant or animal and are called by some scientists the protista. The plant kingdom supposedly evolved into different phyla but we won't follow that story in this lesson. The simple animals began to vary and some started developing a tough cord down one side. They are called the chordata. Some remained simple creatures but others developed a backbone. The first animals with a spinal column were fishes. Some of them remained fishes while others became amphibians. Part of the amphibians developed into reptiles. Some reptiles remained reptiles but others changed still more, some becoming birds and some becoming mammals.

45

Some of the mammals became herbivores and some became carnivores. The carnivores divided into several families, one of which is the canidae or dogs and their close relatives. One genus of the canidae is called Canis. Dogs used by man in that genus were given the species name familiaris. One could trace the supposed ancestry of the house fly in a similar way. Looking at the "tree" we see the common ancestor of the dog and the fly would be some simple organism in the prehistoric ocean. The common ancestor of the dog and cat would be a very recent mammal, but the ancestor of mammals and insects would be very remote .

Let us examine Chart No. 3 which represents part of the "tree" leading to man. The dotted lines represent unknown supposed ancestors. No evolutionist believes that any modern fish is the ancestor of the amphibians nor does he believe the ancestors of any of the phyla are in existence today. He goes to the fossils to find the missing ancestors but he still finds them missing. Let us see what some of the scientists say:

"We shall probably never know what the first chordates were like, because it is unlikely that adequate indications of them are preserved in the fossil record." 1

"The primitive, mammal-like reptiles of the Mesozoic gave rise to a variety of forms from among which some hypothetical ancestor at the end of the Cretaceous period or the beginning of the Eocene gave rise to the placental animals."

From these two quotations we learn that the ancestors of certain groups are unknown. Let us note some more general quotations.

"The idea that the simpler forms of today are forerunners of the more complex forms must be rejected in favor of the idea that the species of today are end products of branches that separated far back in the distant past, and that each one has evolved in its own direction to its present position since it diverged from other species." 3

"There remains, however, the point that for still higher categories discontinuity of appearance in the records is not only frequent but also systematic. Some break in continuity always occurs in categories from orders upwards, at least, although the break may not be large or appear significant to most students." 4

According to Anthony Standen: "The genealogical trees intended to show how modern animals are evolved are familiar enough. If they show any animal as descended from any particular animal (except in a very few restricted lines) they are fudged. Animals are not descended from actual animals, only from hypothetical 'ancestors'. The trees will show a number of branches, and on the tips of the branches will be man, the great apes, the other mammals, and perhaps if it is a comprehensive tree there will be birds, reptiles, amphibians, fish and possibly other things. There ought to be a whole series of animals, going up the main trunk, and out along all the branches, up to the tips where the modern animals are to be found. There aren't any. Haskel's trees have indeed fallen to pieces, for the wood that should support them was all hypothetical wood. And yet they keep on making their appearance in book after book intended for instruction." 5

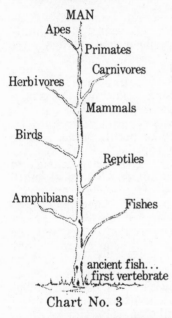

Chart No. 3

Chart No. 3 illustrates what these scientists are saying. The dotted lines represent the missing links or the hypothetical ancestors. By hypothetical ancestors is meant imaginary animals for which there is no evidence that they ever existed. It is the type of creature the evolutionist assumes must have existed.

Mayr in discussing differences between man and anthropoids (apes and their relatives) says the following:

"These characteristics a r e striking and make for a pronounced gap between man and the anthropoids. Yet the theory of evolution demands that man and these anthropoids have descended from a common ancestor. 6

The common ancestor which the theory of evolution demands is missing both in fossil and in living evidence.

The portion of the evolutionary tree shown in Chart No. 3 is the vertebrate branch. Ancient, extinct fishes are supposed to be the first vertebrates. Some of these fishes changed form until they became the thousands of kinds of fishes we have today. Some other ancient fish changed form until it became the first amphibian. Similarly some amphibians became reptiles and the process supposedly continued on up to man. But most of these transitional forms are missing both in fossil records and among present day animals. All fossils as well as living forms fall into one or another of the major classifications. Note that Simpson (an outstanding evolutionist) states definitely that from orders on up the fossil evidence indicates definite classifications. That is there are

47

no halfway animals connecting the major classifications. *This is an important point.* If there are no in-between animals then evolution could not have occured.

Evolutionists recognize the seriousness of these gaps so far as evolutionary theory is concerned and have proposed several theories to explain them. Simpson feels that probably the transition organisms were few in number and evolved rapidly so that few fossils were formed. Also, the rapidly evolving creatures may have lived in restricted areas which man has not searched for fossils. Therefore the fossils have not been found. 7

Creationists feel the fossils have not been found simply because they never existed. The classifications always have been distinct.

It is well at this point to discuss two important so-called links among the fossils. The extinct bird, archeopteryx, is considered evidence that birds evolved from reptiles. The creature had teeth and a long bony tail but it was covered with feathers. It was a true bird with a few reptile-like peculiarities. There was a tremedous gap between it and reptiles. It always has been classified as a bird. The lobefinned fishes are considered links between the fishes and the amphibians. The coelocanth is a modern lobe-finned fish discovered off the coast of Africa in recent years. It has been found in fossil form in Europe and was considered to have been extinct for millions of years. These fishes are considered links between the fishes and the amphibians. They had bones in their fins that were similar to those in the limbs of terrestrial animals. Both the bird and the lobefinned fishes are considered links between phyla. In both cases scientists did not classify them as new phyla but each was placed in one of the major classifications. Even if they are links, there still are many links on each side of them that are not represented by fossils.

Although we find all animals falling definitely in one group or another from phylum through order, the situation is different in the lower categories. (Refer to the classification of the dog.) Darwin called his famous book, *The Origin of Species*. He attempted to show how new species might arise. His theory, and that of later evolutionists, was that if new species could arise, then genera, families, and all other categories could arise in the same way.

The term species has never been accurately defined by scientists. The simplest definition might be that a species is a kind of organism the individuals of which freely breed among themselves and with no other species, and produce fertile offspring. They must resemble each other rather closely; that

is they can be distinguished from other species. This definition is not entirely accurate since we have cases where two
different species do cross, and sometimes, though not usually,
the offspring are fertile.

Scientists attempt to prove ways evolution could have
taken place by producing new species. In some cases, though
rarely, new species have been produced. But in the main the
attempts were failures. In 1928 a scientist named Karpechenko
crossed a cabbage and a radish and got a fertile hybrid. But
the radish and the cabbage belong to the mustard family. Such
different types as roses and cabbages could not be crossed.
Where two different species cross they must be very similar
in structure. So we see the term species is indefinite and
crosses can occur producing new types which occasionally are
fertile. We have to remember that systems of classification
are man-made.

It is claimed by evolutionists that if small changes such
as can be observed occur, then it is logical to assume that
accumulations of small changes over the ages result in greater
changes. This is not the case. For example: not uncommonly
two dark haired parents have a blond child. This is because
both parents are car-
rying the hidden re-
cessive gene for blond
hair. There is no
change in the genes
themselves. Such
minor changes do not
accumulate to produce
such different ani-
mals as fishes and
cows.

Relating to the Bible

The problem of classification is quite important as we
study the relationship between scientific theory and the Bible.
Evolutionists believe life started as a single cell in some ancient
ocean and then evolved or changed into the many forms we
have today. Christians believe God created all living things
and they reproduced after their kind. But we see from scientific evidence that species apparently have changed in some instances. Also, we learned the scientists do not have an exact
definition of species. How do we explain the change in species
when scripture tells us the living things reproduced after their
"kind"? The question hinges on the word "kind" as it is used
in Genesis. There is no way of knowing what the word means
in terms of modern biological classification schemes. It could
have meant phylum, subphylum, class, order, or possibly family

49

or genus. We just don't know. It is entirely scriptural to believe God created the major groups and then through the centuries some new species did arise. Since paleontological evidence indicates no changes have taken place above at least the classification of order, and since fossil evidence and experimentation indicate the possibility (not certainty) that changes have occurred in species, maybe genera, and possibly even families, it is not unscriptural to believe the "kinds" of Genesis were higher categories in our biological classification scheme. Such creatures still would have reproduced after their "kind". Scripture leaves some leeway for changes within groups to have taken place.

Conclusion

From this lesson we learn that the word "kind" as it is used in Genesis can not be defined in terms of species or any other category of modern biological classification. Neither is there a clear definition of the biological term species. Paleontological and experimental evidence indicates probable changes within the lower categories of species, genera, or even families, but such evidence does not indicate any changes in the higher categories. Therefore what is known about both Paleontology and plant and animal changes does not conflict with what is known about the creation.

SUGGESTED ACTIVITIES

1. Explain why Standen said the wood in the tree of life is hypothetical.

---

2. Explain why Christians can accept a limited amount of evolution in the lower categories of classification.

---

3. Linnaeus classified organisms according to structure. Evolutionists classify according to supposed evolution or according to relationships. The results of the two methods of classification are practically the same. Can you explain this?

....

....

....

....

....

4. Examining the supposed evolution of the vertebrates, state at least two differences between each succeeding pairs of the classes.

    a. Fish to amphibians

        (1) Ex. Fish are covered with scales while amphibians have soft skin.

        (2) ....

    b. Amphibians to reptiles

        (1) ....

        (2) ....

    c. Reptiles to birds

        (1) ....

        (2) ....

    d. Reptiles to mammals

        (1) ....

        (2) ....

    e. Animals (mammals) to man

        (1) ....

        (2) ....

5. Collect pictures of various kinds of dogs, roses, chickens, cows, or people. Mount them together showing the wide variations that occur within a "kind." This would be good on the bulletin board.

6. Make a poster of the hypothetical tree of life. Show by colored ink or dotted lines the part of the tree that is hypothetical. Draw little figures or cut out pictures from magazines of the organisms on the tree. Ideas can be found in library books or text books.

REFERENCES

1. Colbert, Edwin H., *Evolution of the Vertebrates,* John Wiley and Sons, Inc., New York, 1955, p. 5.

2. Woodbury, Angus M., *Principles of General Ecology,* The Blakiston Company, Inc., New York, 1954, p. 354.

3. Ibid., p. 306.

4. Simpson, George Gaylord, *The Major Features of Evolution,* Columbia University Press, New York, 1963, p. 366.

5. Standen, Anthony, *Science is a Sacred Cow,* E. P. Dutton and Company, Inc., New York, 1950, pp. 104, 105.

6. Mayr, Ernst, *Animal Species and Evolution,* Harvard University Press, Cambridge, Massachusetts, 1963, p. 625.

7. Simpson, op. cit., p. 367.

LESSON 7

FOSSILS AND THE AGES

Scripture: Job 40:15-24; Job 41:1-34   God shows His power in the creation of the great beasts, behemoth (the hippopotamus) and leviathan (the crocodile). Fossils give evidence of many great beasts.

The science of geology is divided into two major sections: physical geology and historical geology. Physical geology is the study of the kinds of rocks making up the earth. It includes their arrangement in strata (layers) and the changes that have taken place such as folding or breaking. Mountain building, erosion, and volcanic action are included in physical geology. Historical geology is a study of the fossils in the strata. The term historical is used because the fossils are supposed to reveal the evolutionary history of life. Physical geology is a study of the whole earth while historical geology is restricted to the study of the outer strata—those containing fossils. In this lesson we will learn something about how fossils are used in historical geology and how this is related to the Bible.

What Fossils Are

Fossils are the evidence of ancient life. Many fossils are of extinct forms while many present day species are found in fossilized form. A very few fossils are preserved bodies such as the frozen elephants found in Alaska and Siberia. Some plants are found in an almost perfect state of preservation. Insects are found in amber so beautifully preserved that the most minute details can be seen. However, most fossils do not reveal so much. Some are only bones filled with mineral. Some fossils are minerals or limestone which have replaced the original material. Other fossils are carbon films while others are just imprints or casts. Some shells are preserved in the original form. Tracks found in hardened mud are considered fossils.

By far the greater part of the fossils are of hard parts only. Bones and shells often are fossilized but muscles, skin, hair, etc. are seldom preserved.

Geological Time

A large part of the study of geology is theoretical; that is it is a study of the fossils as evidence of evolution. Since life supposedly started as very simple structures which became more complex, it is believed that the lower strata will contain fossils of simple organisms with successive strata in turn containing successively more complex or advanced forms. Scientists believe that the lower forms are ancestral to the higher forms. Evolutionists estimated how much time they thought would be required for the changes to take place from one-celled organisms to man. Earth time was then divided into two *eons:* the Cryptozoic Eon being that including all time before life began and the Phanerozoic Eon being the time in which life has existed. The Phanerozoic Eon was then divided into three *eras,* the Paleozoic (old life) Era, the Mesozoic (middle life) Era, and the Cenozoic (new life) Era. Eras were divided into *periods* which in turn were divided into *epochs*. (See Chart 5) The number of years assigned to the period vary with different scientists. The reason of course is due to the uncertainties of dating as discussed in Lesson 5 as well as the different estimates of the supposed rate of evolution.

The Evidence of the Fossils

Douglas Dewar emphasized the importance of the fossils:

"The theory of organic evolution must stand or fall according as the evidence of the fossils is for it or against it".

Dewar opposed evolution. Carl O. Dunbar, an evolutionist and a paleontologist, has a similar thing to say:

"Although the comparative study of living animals and plants may give very convincing circumstantial evidence, fossils provide the only historical, documentary evidence that life has evolved from simpler to more complex forms." 2

If evolution is true one would expect to find a continuous series of fossils beginning with the simplest to the most complex. One might compare the series to a series of pictures taken one each day from birth until old age. There would be no appreciable difference between any two consecutive pictures but over a period of years great changes would be evident. The fossil series may be compared to pictures taken perhaps once every eight or ten years. See Chart 4 and Chart 5.

The sudden appearance of major groups of organisms is a matter of concern to evolutionists. First a large number of kinds of animals suddenly appear in Cambrian rocks with virtually no fossils in lower rocks. (Recently some vague fossils have been found in Australia and Canada which are thought to be Precambrian.) Note what Dunbar says:

"Although exceedingly rare in the pre-Cambrian rocks, fossils appear in abundance at the base of the Cambrian".

Another puzzling sudden appearance is that of the flowering plants. Again from Dunbar:

"Deciduous trees suddenly become conspicuous in the early Cretacous." 4

The insects are another group which suddenly appeared:

"Hundreds of species of insects are known from Pennsylvanian rocks. This is in strange contrast to the paucity of insect fossils to be found in the Mississippian, and points to a long period of evolution which left no record." 5

It is these sudden appearances of groups of organisms along with the sudden extinctions of groups that provided the basis of division of geological time into eras, periods, and epochs. Again we will refer to Dunbar:

"Since life on the Earth has been continuously evolving, the faunas and floras preserved as fossils provide a basis for Chronology; but if the record were complete they might show gradual change and yet afford no basis for subdivision of the record. The changes have not been gradual however. At certain times, as at the end of each era, extinctions of dominant groups of organisms have occurred within a relatively short span of time and other groups have rapidly expanded to take their place. To a lesser extent this is true of the ends of the several periods of time." 6

So we see geological time as determined by the paleontologist is based on the "missing links."

"Evolution of Man"

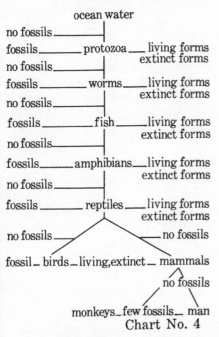

Chart No. 4

Circular Reasoning

There are two ways scientists attempt to determine the position of a fossil in evolutionary sequence. One is by the structure of the fossils and the other by placement in the strata of the earth. Theoretically the first organisms to evolve will be found in fossil form in the lowest fossiliferous layers. Then in succeeding strata will be found succeedingly more advanced organisms. See Chart No. 5. A quotation from Dunbar will help explain this:

"The relative time of existence of a vast number of kinds of animals and plants has now been established and their place in the geologic column has been confirmed by the cooperation of geologists the world over. This is not a theory derived a priori [without experimental evidence], but a discovery painfully and tediously worked out by the systematic study of the faunas of rock formations carefully located in the geologic column. It is an important natural law that *fossil faunas and floras succeed one another in a definite and determinable order*." 7

Mr. Dunbar further says the following:

"— no single area contains a record of all geological time, and if it did, the section would be so thick that its base would be buried beyond our reach; but deposition has always been going on in one place or another, and we need only discover and correlate enough of the scattered fragments to build up a composite record of all geologic time. For more than a hundred years the geologists of all countries have been cooperating in this endeavor, and the total thickness of the stratified rocks now recognized would exceed 500,000 feet (95 miles) if all the beds were directly superposed." 8

The "definite and determinable order" Mr. Dunbar mentions is the evolutionary order. Paleontologists arranged the sequence from strata found in many localities. At any one place only a few formations will be found. Not always are the formations in consecutive order according to evolutionary theory. Often one or more evolutionary stages will be missing. But the strata are dated according to the kind of fossils present.

The geologist uses circular reasoning. He says the simplest organisms will be found on the lowest strata because they evolved first. Then he assigns an early date to any stratum containing simple fossils regardless of its position in the sequence in the immediate locality or of the nature of the rock itself. First he uses strata to date fossils and then he uses fossils to date strata.

Strata

Earth time as discussed previously is divided into two eons. The Cryptozoic Eon (also called Precambrian) represents the greater part of earth time according to theory. During that time the core of the earth made up of metamorphic rocks was formed. Only a few evidences of life are found in Precambrian rocks and some of these fossils are doubtful. In Canada and Australia have been found some supposed fossils.

Above the Precambrian are found the strata containing fossils. As learned earlier the cambrian contains an abundant supply of varied fossils representing all the invertebrate phyla.

Eras	Periods	Typical Animals
Cenozoic Era 70 million yrs.	Quaternary Tertiary	
Mesozoic Era 200 million yrs.	Cretaceous Jurassic Triassic	
Paleozoic Era 330 million yrs	Permian Pennsylvanian Mississippian Devonian Silurian Ordovician Cambrian	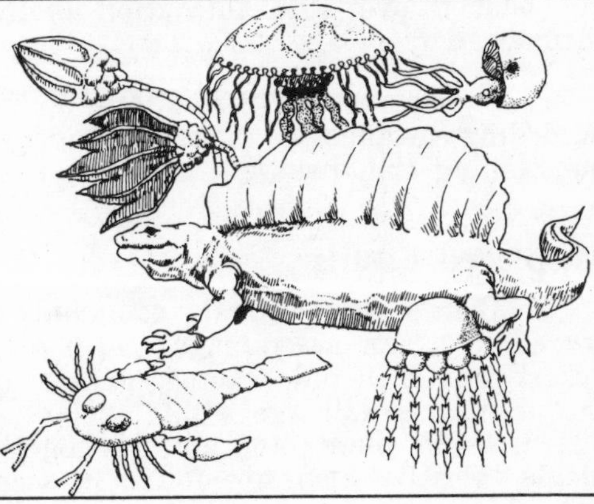
	Precambrian	

Chart No. 5

Referring to Chart No. 5 the student can see the successive strata from the Precambrian to recent. Theoretically the earth should be a vast sphere with the successive strata arranged in layers one above the other in the same order at any one place on the globe. Such is not the case. At no place have all the epochs been found. Surface exposures may be anything from Precambrian to recent. Usually only a few epochs are represented and it is not rare for them not to be in theoretical consecutive order. Either some strata are missing or they are in reversed order.

In the Grand Canyon is an example of missing strata. On the Precambrian rocks is found a Cambrian layer but above is found Devonian rocks. Both the Ordovician and Silurian are missing. Above the Devonian is found the Mississippian in correct order but the Pennsylvanian is missing between that and the Permian. No other geological layers are above the Permian. Geologists are puzzled about the missing strata and explain only that they must have eroded away. 9

The Rocky Mountains area provides an example of up-side-down formations. A Precambrian formation about two miles thick lies on top of Cretaceous rocks. This formation, found in Glacier National Park, is only one of many such examples. Geologists explain this by saying the formation got pushed over the formation under it. This is called a thrust. 10

So we see the formations do not occur as they should according to theory. This provides scientific grounds for questioning the theory.

Misplaced Fossils

Plants and animals commonly found together are referred to as an assemblage. A plant assemblage on a Texas desert would include cactus, greasewood, and mesquite while the animal assemblage would include snakes, desert rats, and lizards. The plants and animals together make a biotic assemblage. Fossils, also, are found in assemblages. A Cretaceous assemblage will be very different from a Devonian assemblage, and Devonian fossils will be different from Eocene specimens. In the man these distinctions are quite evident. Although each formation has its characteristic assemblage, there are many fossils that are found in more than one formation. For example, cockroaches are found in Pennsylvanian formations as well as several others.

But what is the attitude when a specimen is found in a formation which is supposed to be much earlier than the level at which the fossil ordinarily is found? Or to put it another way, the fossil is in the wrong assemblage. Sometimes that happens. Leaves of plants like our modern flowering plants (angiosperms) suddenly appear in Cretaceous rocks. Andrews says in regard to this:

"In explanation of this apparent sudden appearance of the angiosperms most botanists have supposed that they actually originated much earlier than the record indicates, but for one reason or another the forerunners of the group were not preserved." 11

From this we learn that the ancestors of the angiosperms are not known. If they should be found they would be expected to be in earlier formations. The leaves of the angiosperms would be different. Some leaves have been found in Triassic and Jurassic rocks. But they were not like presumed ancestors but appear to be angiosperm leaves. But since they were found in assemblages where they were not supposed to be, paleontologists were hesitant to consider them angiosperms. The scientists hesitated to classify the fossils according to their structure because their location in the rocks did not harmonize with evolutionary theory. 12

Perhaps another more easily understood illustration is the finding of human tracks in the same rocks in which dinosaur tracks are found in the Paluxy River bed near Glenrose, Texas. 13 People weren't supposed to live when dinosaurs lived. Evolutionists reject the evidence of the human foot prints while accepting the dinosaur tracks as valid fossils, even though the human tracks appear just as genuine as the animal tracks. According to the evolutionary hypothesis humans could not have lived at the time of the dinosaurs.

These two examples show how much the interpretations of factual evidence are colored by bias. Evidence is rejected because it does not fit the theory. In the main the assemblages of the various formations run fairly true but there are enough exceptions to cause the evolutionist real concern. These irregularities do not bother the creationists.

Conclusions

From this lesson we learned that fossils are evidences of ancient life. Some of the fossils are of extinct forms while many of them are of present day species. Fossils are the basis for the division of geological time into eras, periods, and epochs with the breaks (missing links) forming the basis for the divisions. The fossils provide the only evidence that evolution may have taken place, but the gaps in the record effectively separate major classifications. These classifications could be the "kinds" of Genesis. The geologist reasons in a circle when he uses position on strata to date fossils and then uses fossils to date strata.

Fossils occur in assemblages which are groups of kinds usually found together. These assemblages run fairly true but not uncommonly the strata with their characteristic assemblages are missing in a sequence or are out of order. The entire geological column is based on evolutionary theory. The irregularities in the sequences suggest that the geological column is lacking at least to that extent in scientific proof.

The Christian does not have to be disturbed by so called fossil evidences. The fossil evidence that the world was once very different from now does not contradict scripture, and the gaps in the records provide a basis for the "kinds" of Genesis.

SUGGESTED ACTIVITIES

1. It has been said that if there had been no fossils there would have been no theory of evolution. Do you agree? Explain.

----

2. Explain why Dewar and Dunbar said fossils offer the only true evidence of evolution.

----

3. Explain the importance of the missing fossils to the evolutionist.

----

4. Explain the importance of the reversed strata or fossils in the wrong order.

----

5. Why are evolutionists concerned about fossils in the wrong strata?

....

....

....

6. Explain how the gaps in the fossil record can explain the "kinds" of Genesis.

....

....

....

....

7. Why do Christians not have to be concerned by fossil evidences?

....

....

....

....

8. Bring some fossils to class. Explain how they likely were formed. List three facts one can learn about them.

    a..

    b..

    c..

List three assumptions one might make about them.

    a..

    b..

    c..

9. If a museum is near, visit it and examine the fossils.

10. The entire class might make a fossil hunting trip. Take a picnic lunch and enjoy Christian fellowship while learning about fossils.

REFERENCES

1. Dewar, Douglas, *The Transformist Illusion*, De Hoff Publications, Murfreesboro, Tennessee, 1957, p. 13.
2. Dunbar, Carl O., Historical Geology, Second Edition, John Wiley and Sons, Inc., New York, 1960, p. 47.
3. Ibid., p. 116.
4. Ibid., p. 332.
5. Stovall, J. Willis and Brown, Howard E., *The Principles of Historical Geology*, Ginn and Company, New York, 1955, p. 267.
6. Dunbar, op. cit., p. 13.
7. Ibid., p. 9.
8. Ibid, p. 9, 10.
9. Ibid., p. 80.
10. Stovall, op. cit., p. 146.
11. Andrews, Henry N., *Studies in Paleobotany*, John Wiley and Sons, Inc., New York, 1961, p. 169.
12. Ibid., p. 169-170.
13. Whitcomb, John C., Jr. and Henry M. Morris, *The Genesis Flood*, Baker Book House, Grand Rapids, 1961, pp 173-175.

LESSON 8

GEOLOGY AND THE FLOOD

Scripture: Gen. 7, 8:1-19; II Pet. 3:3-7   Peter prophesied truly when he said some would scoff.

Before studying the scientific part of this lesson the student should read the account of the flood in Gen. 7, 8:1-19.

In II Pet. 3:3-7 is found a prophecy that people would scoff and would "deliberately ignore" (RSV) the creation, the flood and the promised judgment.   Today the flood ranks with the creation as a portion of the Bible that is disbelieved and considered only a myth or legend.   In this lesson we will consider some aspects of the relation of the account of the flood found in scripture with modern historical geology.   The subject is very involved and we will be able to touch only the high points.

Uniformitarianism Versus Catastrophism

Looking carefully at the prophecy in II Pet. 3:4 we find the scoffers would say, " . . . all things continue as they were from the beginning of the creation."   That is a Biblical expression for the doctrine of uniformitarianism which is the basic principle of modern historical geology.   James Hutton, of Scotland, published a book, *Theory of the Earth,* in 1785. In this book he stated, "The present is key to the past."   By this he meant such geological processes as erosion and volcanic

activity which are taking place now have been taking place
since time started. It is called the "doctrine of uniformitarianism" because all these processes have been uniform or have
continued in the same way for eons of time. This doctrine
eliminates the Biblical point of view about geology. This view
is called "catastrophism" because the great flood was a catastrophe. The two points of view are contradictory.

These two contradictory ideas are of great importance
to the Christian who accepts the Bible. The geologist offers
a wealth of evidence in favor of his theory and makes it quite
convincing. The Christian accepts the Bible on the basis of
a quite different kind of· evidence. Can the rocks offer evidence of the truth of scripture? Let us examine some phases
of the problem by first noting the high points of the two
philosophies.

Catastrophism Biblical	Uniformitarianism Scientific
1. God created the heavens and the earth.	1. Stars and planets formed from gases and/or energy. No source proposed.
2. God created living things after their kinds.	2. Living things originated by spontaneous generation and by evolution changed into many kinds.
3. God destroyed life a n d changed the earth's sur-face by a great flood. (Catastrophe).	3. For some 4½-6 billion years the earth has been going through geological changes. (Uniformity)
4. Fossils could have been formed as a result of the flood.	4. Fossils formed over long period of time as result of natural processes.
5. Earth before the flood probably was very differ-ent from earth of today. Climate and living things different.	5. Changes in the earth and its inhabitants have been gradual over billions of years.

Christians certainly do not deny the presence of fossils
nor the kind of prehistoric life they indicate. Neither do they
deny that the earth's strata indicate some sort of great events
in times past. Also even though there are missing strata and
reversed strata and fossils are found out of their usual or
expected locality, in the main fossils do occur in assemblages
with distinct characteristics. It is not the presence of these
things that causes the trouble. It is the interpretation which
is contradictory.

Again, as in the case of the creation, God did not see
fit to give us much detail. Let us see what is revealed. First,

we note two sources of the water: from the windows of heaven and from the deep. That is, the water came from the air above and from the ground below. It is useless to try to explain how the water arose. As to the quantity we are told all the mountains were covered to a depth of fifteen cubits. There was no land left uncovered. The rains continued for forty days. The water prevailed after the rain stopped for one hundred and fifty days and then the ark rested on Mt. Ararat. The waters continued to recede until the earth was dry some eleven months after the beginning of the rain. The waters remained on the earth for a long time. It is easy to imagine that much water being able to do a tremendous amount of changing of the surface of the earth.

There is much evidence of flood conditions on the earth. First, fossils are found in all parts of the world—even on high mountains and beneath artic ice. Most of the fossils are of water animals though plants and land animals certainly are found. The presence of such fossils indicates that at least at one time the land was covered by water. Often the condition of the fossils suggests sudden catastrophic burial. Enormous quantities of one kind of fossils are commonly found in one formation. Both young and adults are found together. Often skeletons of fishes, especially, are found complete. Not uncommonly their position indicates they were violently moving as though trying to escape some great danger. According to evolutionary theory these organisms died and were buried by sediment washing in. When fishes die in nature they quickly get eaten by other creatures. The bones fall apart and are scattered. They don't die in such enormous numbers at once.

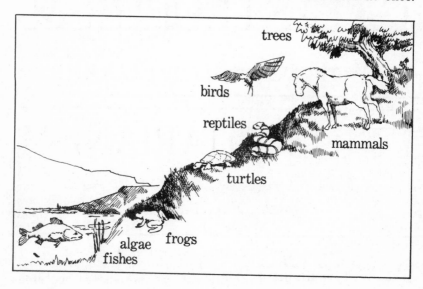

These evidences of catastrophic amounts of water do not prove the Biblical flood, but they merely suggest there have been great amounts of water on the earth, and this can be accounted for by the flood of scripture. There could have been local floods in addition to the Biblical flood. Uniformitarian theory includes the movements of great seas but they were gradual movements. Also local floods are postulated by uniformitarians.

The belief in catastrophism can include volcanic action. In many regions of the earth, especially in western United States, are found enormous amounts of lava. Igneous rocks indicate great heat at some time. These igneous rocks often form layers called sills that are found between strata of sedimentary rock.

Not only are both sedimentary and igneous rocks found in various thicknesses and order but often they are broken, buckled, folded, or cracked. This is easily seen along roadside cuts. Evidently great changes took place in the earth's crust at some time. Geologists explain these things as being great changes which took place over long periods of time. The theory of uniformitarianism will not entirely explain these things. Note what Morris and Whitcomb say:

"Uniformitarianism, in other words, has simply been assumed, not proved. Catastrophism has simply been denied, not refuted." 1

CATASTROPHISM

World Destroyed by FLOOD

UNIFORMITARIANISM

Natural processes account for all geological changes...

The present condition of the earth is quite evident. How it got that way is a matter of theory. The geologists who believe in uniformitarianism say natural movements occurred in the remote past which were similar to the earthquakes and volcanic action of today. Sedimentary formations are believed to have been produced by floods or by the work of melting glaciers during the ice age. In reality the geologist has no absolute proof. The Christian believes in a great catastrophe in the form of flood which took place in the time of Noah. The Bible describes such a flood in briefest terms though it does not specifically mention volcanic action. There are indications of activity that may have been volcanic.

Again looking at II Pet. 3:6 we find that Peter said, "The world that *then was* . . . " This is a direct implication that the world of today is different from the world before Noah. Fossil evidence certainly indicates the world once was different. According to a chart from Easton: of a total of 1,135,000 known species of animals, 130,000 are extinct and 1,105,000 are living. 2 These figures are in round numbers and new species, both living and fossil, are being discovered as time goes by. However, these figures indicate a large number of extinct forms. In the field of botany, also, there are many species of extinct forms. Many of the extinct forms look very queer compared to modern types. Not only are the organisms different but many of them belonging in mild climates are found in the artic regions. In other words much of the fossil evidence indicates a time when the climate was mild. Undoubtedly at one time the earth was different from what it is today. In this respect fossil evidence and scripture seem to harmonize.

Attempted Harmonizations

The *Gap Theory* mentioned in Lesson 5 is one attempt to explain fossils and geological strata in the light of scripture. The statement was made in the first verse of Genesis that God created the heavens and the earth. Then follows a description of six days on which God organized the earth, created or made plant and animal life, and created man. Some Christians believe the period between Genesis 1:1 and the rest of the chapter may have been millions of years long. Since God does not say how long that time was it does scripture no violence to believe a long period occurred at that point. Some scholars believe the Hebrew word translated "was" can just as accurately be translated "became" in Gen. 1:2. If "became" is the correct translation, then the earth must have gone through a deterioration of some sort before the six days started. Some believe there was life on the earth at that time and fossils were formed during that period. This theory does not contradict the Bible. According to this theory the geological ages described could have taken place and then were followed by the six days.

66

The *Long Days Theory* has been proposed by some. They believe the six days really were long periods of time. This allows for the geological ages. In favor of this theory is the fact that sun, moon, and stars were created as means of giving light on the fourth day. They measure our present days and seasons. The first three days were not measured in the way days are measured now. There are arguments against long days. One is the use of the expression "day and night" which implies ordinary days such as we know. Also linguists say that the use of a number, such as "first", "second", etc. before the word "day" indicates the word meant one twenty-four hour day as we know it. In our study of ecology in a later lesson we will learn more about the unlikelihood of long days.

It should be remembered that both the *Long Day Theory* and the *Gap Theory* are attempts on the part of some to accept both the Bible and evolutionary hypothesis regarding time. Scripture in no way suggests either theory; it merely is silent on the matter of dates. However, to accept the evolutionist's concept of long periods of time, might in effect let the gate down to complete evolutionary philosophy. Scripture does not say when the universe was created and science has no way of finding out. Christians will do well to leave the matter there.

Plant Life Following the Flood

The account of the flood in Genesis was not meant as a lesson in geology but is a part of the record of God's dealing with man. The account is very sketchy so far as the catastrophe is concerned. We are told the source of the water, how extensive it was, and the duration of the flood. Particularly noticeable is the lack of reference to plants. No provision was made for their preservation. Yet there were plants on the land after the flood. The dove found an olive leaf. Besides this evidence, it can be inferred that plants were present. How else could the people and animals from the ark obtain food? For plants to grow soil must be present. Soil consists of pulverized rock and minerals plus a tremendous amount of organic matter both living and decaying. Bacteria, molds, protozoa, algae, worms, and insects are found in soil. The dead plant and animal matter decays and the substances are returned to the soil to maintain its fertility. Plants will not grow in pulverized rock alone. Possibly some of the soil was buried and became shale, a kind of rock containing organic matter. Some of the soil may have been heaped up in places and left. Seeds or plant roots or stems could have started growing there. No one knows how the plants were preserved or possibly even re-created, and to try to explain is speculation. Speculation easily can be erroneous. It is enough for the creationist to accept the Biblical account and not try to explain how God preserved the plants.

Summary

In the geological strata there are many evidences of a different earth and of great changes having taken place. Some are difficult to explain by a flood alone. Lava beds, especially in western United States, point to volcanic action of a magnitude beyond anything known in history. The frozen mammoths are unmistakable evidence of a sudden great cold. Scripture does not explain these things.

Many people of today scoff at the idea of a great flood and state that the earth has gone through a great series of changes without interruption by a flood. This is called "uniformitarianism." Christians believe in a great flood which may have been accompanied by other catastrophic events such as volcanic action. This is called "catastrophism." The earth shows evidence of great changes both in life and in the surface of the earth. There are weaknesses in the scientific theories concerning fossils and strata. All efforts to harmonize scripture and scientific theories are theories themselves and not subject to verification. The Christian accepts the Bible in its entirety and does not become disturbed by theories. He remembers that God expects him to believe and that God explains only what is necessary for his salvation. It is not necessary that we understand about fossils or strata. From Handrich we have these words:

"Let there be doubts about human theories, and also about those theories which are intended to harmonize with the Bible; but let the Word of God itself remain as a solid rock in the midst of the shifting theories." 3

SUGGESTED ACTIVITIES

1. List some things scripture does not explain about the flood.

    a...

    b...

    c...

2. List some facts scripture does tell about the flood.

    a...

    b...

    c...

3. What are some evidences of great catastrophes other than the flood?

a. ....

b. ....

c. ....

4. Explain why it is not unscriptural to accept the idea of other catastrophes besides the flood.

....

....

....

5. What Biblical evidence suggests that the world once was very different? (See also Gen. 2:6)

....

....

....

....

6. Explain why the "days" of creation play such an important part both in the account of the creation and in the record of the flood.

....

....

....

....

....

7. Examine the strata in a roadside cut, in a quarry, or on a mountain side. Note the colors, texture, thickness, and breaks or folds. Explain how you think the flood may have formed the strata.

....

....

....

....

8. If there are fossils in the strata, see if you can find different kinds in different layers. Explain.

----

9. Place a mixture of gravel, coarse sand, and fine soil in a jar. Add water and shake. Observe the "strata" formed as the contents settle.

10. Press leaves, shells, or bones in soft plaster of Paris. Let the plaster of Paris harden. Remove the objects. The remaining imprint will illustrate how some fossils must have been formed in soft mud which hardened.

REFERENCES

1. Whitcomb, John C. Jr. and Henry M. Morris, *The Genesis Flood*, Baker Book House, Grand Rapids, Michigan, 1961. p. 137.

2. Easton, W. H., *Invertebrate Paleontology*, Harper and Brothers, Publishers, New York, 1960, p. 5.

3. Handrich, Theodore L., *The Creation*, Moody Press, Moody Bible Institute, Chicago 60610, 1953, p. 116.

LESSON 9

PHYSICAL EVIDENCES

Scripture I Cor. 15:35-45 Paul definitely states that animals are different. Evolutionists emphasize similarities instead of differences.

Evolutionists believe that after the first living cells appeared in the ocean living organisms went through a long series of changes from one form to another until present day plants and animals and man appeared. They find what they consider evidence from several sources. In this lesson we will consider evidence found in physical structures and chemical composition.

Homologous Organs

Evolutionists consider similarities of structure of plants and animals as evidences of relationship and of descent from a common ancestor. Since animals are more familiar to the student we will use them as a means of illustration though

70

plants also show many similarities. The study of such similarities is called *comparative anatomy* and similar organs are said to be *homologous*.

The easiest illustration to use and one frequently seen in biology books is the similarities of the fore limbs of the higher animals or vertebrates. The vertebrates include the fishes, amphibians, reptiles, birds, and mammals. We find all of their fore limbs except those of the fishes constructed on a common pattern.

The sizes and shapes of these bones vary widely. In a bird's wing it is easy to find the upper limb bone and the two lower limb bones but the third part of the wing bears little resemblance to the hand of a person or the foot of a horse. An anatomist can find the similar structures however. The horse walks on the middle toe only and the hoof is the toe nail. A pig walks on two toes and two other toes are situated at the back of the foot and are not used for walking. In the bat the fingers are extremely long with folds of skin between them which the animal uses for flying. There are animals with long toenails or claws such as the cats while others such as the mole have fore limbs made for digging. The whale is an animal whose fore limbs are made into great paddles to propel it through water. With all these variations the bones are similar in number and arrangement.

Similar comparison could be made with the hind limbs, the ribs and backbone, the skull, or any other part of the body. Evolutionists believe the similarities are evidence that the animals are related and that they had common ancestors. They say that if God created each kind of animal He would have created each on a different pattern. Creationists believe that God created such animals on a similar pattern simply because that kind of structure works best. He varied the details to suit the way the animal lives. Creationists argue that similarity simply indicates one Creator instead of common ancestry.

Evolutionists study similarities and differences in cell structure, chemical composition of the body, especially the blood, and other phases of body structure and composition. Many times they find discrepancies. For example the composition of the blood might indicate animal A is closely related to Animal B while skeletal structure would lead some to believe animal A is more closely related to animal C. This produces a problem for the evolutionist.

Embryology

The study of the developing young before birth is called *embryology*. This field has been considered very important as a source of proof that evolution took place as well as the

71

stages by which it supposedly occurred. It has been found that developing vertebrate embryos go through somewhat similar stages during the early days or weeks. Even in these early stages however, one is able to distinguish between fish, cat, bird, or human embryos. This similarity is considered by evolutionists evidence that the animals evolved from a common ancestor. Note what Moody has to say:

"The common pattern of embryonic development seems most reasonably explained as having been inherited from an ancestor common to all the animals possessing the similar embryonic developments. Explanations not involving common ancestry may take two forms. It may be maintained that the Creator created each species separately but saw fit to confer on different species similar processes of embryonic development. Or it may be maintained that mechanical and physiological necessities operating in development bring about the similarities—that there is, in effect, no other road which an ovum could follow in its development to the adult stage." 1

Moody states that the most reasonable explanation is the evolutionary one—that is, the animals inherited common structure from a common ancestor. Creationists accept the second explanation—that is, God just willed to make the animals that way. The third explanation is not in any sense unchristian. Perhaps each animal in its development does so by the simplest, easiest route.

Many books carry drawings of embryos of several animals such as fish, birds, and man, showing supposed similarities. They are copied from the drawings proposed by Ernest Haeckel and are supposed to provide evidence of evolution. Some recent books have changed the drawings since evolutionists now recognize Haeckel's drawings were not entirely accurate. This evidence has been abandoned even by many evolutionists themselves.

Another phase of the supposed evidence for evolution found in embryological development is the recapitulation theory. Ernest Haeckel stated the theory in this way: "Ontogeny recapitulates phylogeny." What he meant was: The stages of development of the embryo (ontogeny) repeats (recapitulates) the evolutionary history of the animal (phylogeny). The human heart, for example, in early stages of development has two chambers, later three chambers are formed, then four chambers with an opening between the right and left sides, and finally the fully formed heart with four separate chambers in the newborn baby. The fish has a two-chambered heart and the frog has a three-chambered heart. The reptile heart has four incomplete chambers while the mammal heart has four chambers. This is considered evidence that some unkonwn extinct fish evolved into an amphibian, an amphibian became a reptile, a reptile became a mammal, and finally man evolved. The developing embryonic heart repeats the history of our ancestors according to this idea. But evolutionists have a problem here. Following the two-chambered stage, the heart becomes a tube for a time before continuing through later stages. This single-tube stage is in the wrong sequence to fit evolutionary theory. William W. Ballard simply states that the idea of heart development recapitulating phylogeny is false. 2 Leslie Brainerd Arey, also, teaches that the theory will not hold up. 3 Both of these men are evolutionists. Even though authors such as these deny the validity of the evidence, drawings of heart series still are common in books students read.

Two other supposed embryonic evidences are the tail and the gill slits. At one stage of development the end of the spine projects, forming a sort of tail. Evolutionists claim this shows we evolved from animals that had tails.

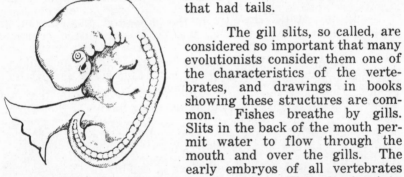

The gill slits, so called, are considered so important that many evolutionists consider them one of the characteristics of the vertebrates, and drawings in books showing these structures are common. Fishes breathe by gills. Slits in the back of the mouth permit water to flow through the mouth and over the gills. The early embryos of all vertebrates have pharyngeal clefts in the neck region. They develop into certain structures in the neck and head. In birds and mammals no slits ever are formed and there is no trace of gills at any stage. According to Ballard the designation "gill slits" is not appropriate. 4 Huettner, also, points out this discrepancy. 5 Even in the fishes there are more pharyngeal clefts in the embryo than gill arches in the adult. The anterior clefts develop into structures other than gills. With all these discrepancies in the evidence, students still are taught that the "gill slits" of the embryo provide evidence that mammals evolved from some sort of fish.

The Christian views these structures as necessary stages in the development of a single cell into a human being. God created man and vertebrate animals with similar body structure. That is, there are four limbs, two ears, and one nose. Since the basic pattern is the same, it is to be expected that the stages in the development of the embryo would be similar and would follow the simplest route.

Haeckel's theory has been modified or changed to some extent. Evolutionists now say the embryo repeats the embryonic form, not the adult form of the ancestors. This does not explain anything since as mentioned above similar structures are to be expected to be formed in similar ways. An important English evolutionist, Sir Gavin de Beer, devotes an entire book to the repudiation of Haeckel's theory. 6 Although evolutionists themselves differ in their attitudes toward the validity of the theory, the idea is very common in evolutionary reading designed for young people.

Vestigial Organs

By vestigial organs is meant structures found in man which are non-functional but do function in some of the animals. The appendix is the best known example of that. In some of the animals such as the rat, it is quite large and serves a digestive function. Scientists themselves disagree as to the significance of the appendix. Moody believes it is clear evidence of evolution. With reference to the appendix he says the following:

"We do not use our caecum and appendix as a container for food undergoing bacterial action. Then why do we have them? The most reasonable explanation seems to be that we inherited them from some remote ancestor having a diet which necessitated such adjuncts to the digestive system. When the descendents of this ancestor eventually changed their food habits the caecum and appendix, no longer useful, decreased in size until they became mere remnants of the functional organs they once had been." 7

Alfred S. Romer, another evolutionist, has a different point of view.

"This is frequently cited as a vestigial organ supposedly proving something or other about evolution. This is not the case; a terminal appendix is a fairly common feature in the caecum of mammals, and is present in a host of primates and a number of rodents. Its major importance would appear to be in the financial support of the surgical profession." 8

Other scientists also question the supposed evolutionary significance of the appendix. Sir Arthur Keith believes it is a functional organ which is not understood yet. Dr. Leon O. Jacobson, with some co-workers did some experimental work with rabbits which indicated the appendix had something to do with the formation of anti-bodies (substances which combat disease).

Some organs once thought to be vestigial and of evolutionary significance are now known to be highly important functional structures. The endocrine glands once were thought to be useless vestiges. Now, much is known about their extremely important secretions, the hormones. Other vestigial organs are the ear muscles which function in animals but not in man, and the third transparent eyelid easily seen in birds and frogs but is only a fold of tissue in man. The tiny hairs on man's body are considered evidence he once was hairy like the apes. The coccyx (bones at the end of the spine) are thought to show we once had a tail. There are many other examples in animals as well as in man which we will not be able to consider in this work.

In view of the fact that some organs formerly thought to be vestigial are now known to be useful, it is reasonable to believe that most likely uses will later be found for those not now understood. In case no use ever is found it may still be due to man's lack of knowledge. Then as we have observed, God created all the vertebrates on a similar pattern with variations to meet the needs of each kind. Perhaps these apparently useless organs are just part of the general similarity.

Conclusion

In this lesson we have considered three kinds of evolutionary evidence. We found that the body structures of the higher animals and man are very much alike. Evolutionists claim that is evidence the animals changed in the ages from one type to another. Creationists say the similarity is evidence of one designer, God. Also it is believed that the form was designed to serve the function. Embryological development is considered proof by the evolutionist that higher animals evolved from lower ones. The creationist simply believes God made it that way and that the stages merely represent the simplest way a single cell can become a complex animal. Then, last, vestigial organs were considered as evolutionary proof. It was found evolutionists themselves differ in their opinions and that some so called vestigial organs have been found to be useful. The Christian accepts God's creation as it is without questioning the reason for structures being as they are.

SUGGESTED ACTIVITIES

1. Explain why the physical evidences discussed in this lesson can not "prove" evolution.

----

2. How do these same evidences suggest a creator?

_____

_____

_____

_____

3. Observe the movements of the fore limbs of a cat, dog, bird, and person. Note how each is designed for the way it functions. Could man improve on this design? Explain.

_____

_____

_____

_____

4. At a hobby shop obtain a model human skeleton. Note how the joints move. Move your own limbs and feel the bones and joints. Note the odd shapes of such bones as the shoulder blade. Study the end of the backbone, the coccyx. This structure, composed of four vertebrae fused together, is considered by the evolutionist to be a shortened tail. There is no fossil evidence of progressively shortened tails. The coccyx in man forms part of the pelvic region of the skeleton and helps hold muscles and connective tissues in place.

5. Find drawings of embryos in several books. Note that even though there is a resemblance, one can easily see the differences between the embryos of different animals. Also, note that the drawings vary in different books.

6. According to Dalcq 9 even the egg cells differ before cell division starts and the very early stages of development differ widely. Ballard 10 states that fins and legs are different from the very beginning with no recapitulation being shown in the embryos. Why do you think these differences are not emphasized, usually not even mentioned, while the similarities are stressed beyond reality?

_____

_____

_____

_____

_____

REFERENCES

1. Moody, Paul A., *Introduction to Evolution,* Second Edition, Harper and Brothers, New York, 1962, p. 47.
2. Ballard, William W., *Comparative Anatomy and Embryology,* The Ronald Press Company, New York, 1964, p. 509.
3. Arey, Leslie Brainerd, *Developmental Anatomy,* W. B. Saunders Company, 1954, p. 7.
4. Ballard, op. cit., p. 75.
5. Huettner, *Comparative Embryology of the Vertebrates,* The McMillan Company, New York, 1949, p. 273.
6. de Beer, Sir Gavin, *Embryos and Ancestors,* Oxford University Press, New York, 1962. (Printed from corrected sheets of third edition, dated 1958).
7. Moody, op. cit., p. 42.
8. Romer, Alfred Sherwood, *The Vetebrate Body,* W. B. Saunders Company, Philadelphia, 1955, p. 379.
9. Dalcq, A. M., *Introduction to General Embryology,* Oxford University Press, London, 1957, p. 32.
10. Ballard, op. cit., p. 426.

LESSON 10
HEREDITY AND EVOLUTION

Scripture: Gen. 1:11-12, 20-22, 27-28; Mat. 7:16-20; Lk. 6:43-45; Mat. 12:33; James 3:12. The principle that each organism produces its own kind is so basic that it is used as a basis for spiritual lessons.

Comparative anatomy is supposed to show the relationship of organisms. Embryology supposedly reveals the history of the evolution of the organism. Paleontology presents theoretical evidence that evolution has taken place. Genetics (the study of heredity) is believed to explain how new types appear. In this lesson we shall study some aspects of the science of genetics and its relation to the Bible.

Chromosomes and Genes

All living things are made up of little units called cells. Each cell is a tiny bit of living material called protoplasm which is surrounded by a thin membrane and contains a small structure in the center called a nucleus. It is the nucleus which is of interest to us in the study of heredity.

When the cell is resting the nucleus is a rounded structure containing chromosomes the structure of which is not very evident because they do not stain well at this stage. When the cell divides the chromosomes change shape and stain better so that they are easily seen. They vary in shape, often being somewhat string-like. The chromosomes occur in identical pairs (except those which determine sex) and a definite number of pairs is found in each species. In man there are twenty-three pairs or forty-six chromosomes. In plants and animals the number varies from one in a certain kind of worm to as many as sixteen hundred in a tiny one-celled animal. Chromosomes in plants also vary in number. The number of chromosomes has nothing to do with the complexity of the organism.

On the chromosomes are found extremely small structures called genes which can be seen only with the electron microscope. Evidence is pretty conclusive that the genes carry the hereditary traits. Estimates of the number of genes present in one cell vary widely but they run into the thousands.

In the reproductive glands are cells which give rise to the eggs in the female and the sperms in the male. In Chart No. 6 the formation of these cells and their union in fertilization are illustrated using only two pairs of lines to represent the chromosomes. Note there are two identical pairs in each beginning cell. When the eggs and sperms are formed the cells divide with one of each pair going to the new cell. Then when

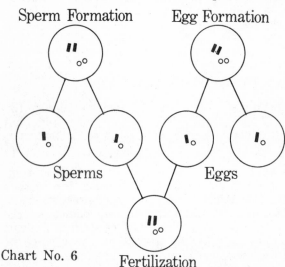

Sperm Formation   Egg Formation

Sperms   Eggs

Chart No. 6   Fertilization

fertilization takes place an egg and a sperm unite to form a fertilized egg. This cell contains one chromosome of each pair from each parent. Thus the new organism inherits equally from each parent. Each member of the pairs of chromosomes carries genes for the same traits as the other member. For example one pair of chromosomes carries the genes which determines the color of eyes. The child inherits one chromosome from the father and one from the mother. Suppose one parent has pure blue eyes and the other has pure brown eyes. The child does not have mixed eyes but has brown eyes but he can pass on blue eyes to his children. The brown eyes show in the hybrid but the blue is covered. The trait which covers another trait is said to be dominant while the hidden trait is said to be recessive. Chart No. 7 illustrates the formation of a hybrid with brown eyes. The dominant trait is written with a capital letter while the recessive trait is written with a small letter. Although the eyes of the hybrid are brown, it is possible for two hybrid people to have a blue-eyed child. Chart No. 7 illustrates this. Notice that when the reproductive cells are formed each parent produces two kinds of cells, one carrying traits for blue eyes and one carrying genes for brown eyes. When fertilization takes place four possible combinations can occur producing pure dominant, pure recessive, and hybrid traits. If the two genes for blue eyes are combined the child will have blue eyes but the other combinations will result in brown eyes.

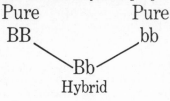

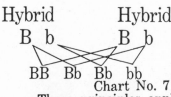

Chart No. 7

These principles apply to both plants and animals and are referred to as Mendel's laws because they were discovered by an Austrian monk named Mendel. This illustration is based on only one trait. There are hundreds of traits in plants and animals which are passed on in this way.

Some recessive traits are not completely hidden by the dominant. Brown hair is dominant over blond hair but the hybrid is likely to be light brown or a shade between that of the parents. This incomplete dominance often is found both in animals and plants.

Mutations

Geneticists have learned by experimenting that the genes on the chromosomes carry hereditary traits. It is the genes that determine the type of plant or animal that results from the union of the two cells, the egg and the sperm. If a change occurs in the genes, even one gene, there is corresponding change in the organism. Also, only changes in genes are passed on to descendants. If a man or woman gets a finger cut off the lack of the finger is not passed on to the child. But if a change in the genes of a parent which determine the kinds of fingers occurs the baby may be born without a finger or it may have extra fingers. In any plant or animal all changes in appearance are caused by changes in genes. This does not include changes such as stunted growth because of lack of food.

Changes that appear without any apparent reason are called "mutations." Sometimes they are called "sports" but that is not a scientific name. It is not known what causes mutations in nature. In laboratories mutations have been caused by radio-active materials, chemicals, and by changes of temperature. These conditions do not exist in the natural world to the degree that is attained in the laboratory. In the laboratory a much higher degree of radiation is produced than ever occurs in nature, and organisms in nature do not contact the chemicals nor extreme temperature changes the scientist produces. Let us see what geneticists have to say about the importance of mutations to evolutionary theory:

"This unique ability of a gene to draw from the surrounding medium the various building blocks needed to duplicate itself and to impress upon them its own pattern, even when that pattern is a changed, or a mutated pattern, is at the very center of the process of the evolution of life." 1

"On this hypothesis a mutation, either natural or induced, is thought of as being an alteration in the chemical arrangement of the molecule. The mutated gene, in its reproduction, duplicates itself in its altered form just as faithfully as it previously copied its original form. This is one of the foundation stones of evolution." 2

Evolutionists believe that it is through mutations that evolution takes place. They think that in some way a gene becomes changed and causes a change in the organism and that change can be passed on to descendants. If the change is beneficial to the organism it will be perpetuated but if it is harmful the organism will be defective or will die.

There are a number of weaknesses in this theory. First, mutations happen very rarely. Geneticists have experimented with fruit flies producing mutations by artificial means. From these studies it is estimated that one fruit fly gene will mutate in nature only once in about one million individuals. 3   To change a reptile to a bird would require a tremendous number of mutations each of which would have to be beneficial to the animal. It is inconceivable that so many advantageous mutations could occur even in the billions of years allowed by the evolutionists.

Still another factor unfavorable to evolutionary theory is the fact that most known mutations are harmful to the organism. The Ancon sheep is an example. In 1791 a man in New England found a lamb in his flock with short bowed legs. Mr. Wright decided this would be an advantage to him since the short legged sheep could not jump over the fence so easily. He bred the lamb to others in his flock and managed to develop a short legged breed. The short legs were an advantage to the farmer but in nature the sheep would be an easy prey to wolves and would not be likely to survive. The mutation was harmful to the sheep. Also, the Ancon sheep did not reproduce very well and eventually died out even with the farmer caring for them. Mutants often can not reproduce at all or if they do it is at a slow rate as in the case of the sheep.

According to Theodosius Dobzhansky mutations in general are harmful with the only known beneficial ones being those occurring in an organism which is not in its normal environment. 4 Dr. William J. Tinkle, a geneticist, says: "Mutations regularly reduce vigor, whatever else they do." (personal communication) The Ancon sheep was kept in existence for a time under the care of man. The environment was not its natural one. Even under these circumstances the sheep did not have enough vigor to maintain its kind. H. J. Muller, one of America's leading geneticists, emphasizes three facts about mutations; namely, (1) they are exceedingly rare, (2) they occur sporadically, and (3) they are practically all harmful. 5 If mutations are not immediately lethal, they reduce the survival capacity of the type so that it eventually becomes extinct.

Still another problem to the evolutionist is the fact that most mutations are recessive. For a recessive trait to appear in offspring both parents must be carrying the same kind of genes for that trait. There are two ways in which this can happen. Either both parents carry the same mutation which they inherited from a common ancestor or the same mutation occurred in each parent. The former situation is far more likely. In either case recessive traits can remain concealed, causing no harm, except in the rare cases when the pure trait occurs.

Chromosome Changes

The student knows that children in a family tend to resemble their parents more than they do other adults. Also, they usually resemble each other more than they do other individuals. That is because they inherit their genes from the same source. They have more of the same kind of genes. However, they inherit from both parents who are hybrid in many respects so they get various combinations. Looking at Chart No. 7 we see the children of two hybrid brown-eyed parents can have blue or brown eyes. Similarly they can have brown, blonde, or red hair. The hair may be curly or straight. There are so many possible combinations that it is estimated there is only one chance in three hundred trillion of any two people, except identical twins, having the same genes. 5

Children in one family resemble each other and their parents because they inherit a high percentage of the same genes but they differ from each other because they do not get exactly the same genes. This principle applies to plants and animals.

Sometimes an individual plant or animal appears which differs from the parent more than is the usual case. The variations can be explained in several ways which have been proven in experimental work. First there is the rearrangement of the genes that occurs every time fertilization takes place. Then sometimes the chromosomes change. Occasionally two companion chromosomes break and exchange ends. Again the chromosomes may break into three parts and exchange the middle parts. There have been known cases where the end of one chromosome broke off and became attached to another chromosome. Sometimes part of a chromosome will become separated from the remainder of the structure. Such changes in chromosomes result in unexpected changes or variations. In some cases, almost always in plants, the number of chromosomes changes, being doubled, tripled, or even quadrupled. This is called polyploidy. As in the case of mutations, which are changes in genes, chromosomal changes usually are harmful, often lethal.

Genetics and Genesis

Hybridization results in a mixing of genes already present. Hybrids within a species are fertile. For example two varieties of cows, the beef cow and the dairy cow, when crossed result in an intermediate type, with some characteristics of both parents. They are the same species. Man has segregated the genes of many domesticated plants and animals producing many varieties useful to himself. The Indians developed the three basic kinds of corn; sweet corn, pop corn, and field corn which man uses today for animal feed as well as for industrial purposes. The Arabs developed the Arabian horse centuries ago. These domesticated varieties freely cross with other types. Plants as different as oaks, elms, and cedars will not cross. Neither will animals that are very different cross. In some cases organisms classified as different genera cross, but we must remember that classification is a man-made thing and scientists do not always agree as to what a genus is.

Both mutations and changes in chromosomes result in changes within the species. Mutations produce new genes but not new species. There is no change known in nature or the laboratory where there was a change in order or any of the higher categories, and known changes in the lower classifications are exceedingly rare. For many years geneticists have experimented with fruit flies and have produced a variety of mutations but the new types still are fruit flies. The "kinds" hold true. The many variations that occur always are within strict limits. There are no known facts about hereditary changes which contradict Genesis.

Conclusion

Genetics is the science of heredity. Mendel's Laws of Heredity hold true for both plants and animals. Evolutionists consider mutation the basis of evolution. Mutations are exceedingly rare and most of them are harmful. That being true it seems that organisms would devolve instead of evolve. Scientists have produced many variations within species and perhaps in some rare instances changed species. At no time have scientists produced new members of the higher categories. Members of the higher classifications do not cross. All of these harmonize with the "kinds" of Genesis. Scientists have not proven evolution by genetics.

SUGGESTED ACTIVITIES

1. Explain the difference between evolution and variation.

....

....

....

....

....

2. Explain why mutation is considered the foundation of evolution.

....

....

....

....

....

3. Give three weaknesses in the theory that mutations cause evolution.

a. ....

b. ....

c. ....

4. In one family several members have a tiny patch of hairs in one eyebrow that grow backward, that is they slant in the wrong direction. This is a harmless mutation. Perhaps you know of a slight abnormality in your own family or in some other family. Describe it.

....

....

....

....

....

5. Do you have any idea whether the mutation is dominant or recessive? If so, explain.

....

....

....

....

6. The tiny patch of hairs growing in the wrong direction is so small very few people even are aware of it. Would that be the case if the entire eyebrow, or even both brows, grew backward? Would it then be considered harmless? Could the mutation be considered beneficial? Explain.

....

....

....

....

7. Describe a mutation that may have occurred in a plant or animal you raised.

....

....

....

....

8. Did any of the mutations you described make the organism stronger or more beautiful? Explain.

REFERENCES

1. Snyder, L. H. and Paul R. David, *The Principles of Heredity*, D. C. Heath and Company, Boston, 1957, p. 377.

2. Ibid., pp. 388, 389.

3. Ibid., p. 350.

4. Dobzhansky, Theodosius, *Evolution, Genetics, and Man*, John Wiley & Sons, Inc., New York, 1955, pp. 105, 106.

5. Muller, H. J., "Redintegration of the symposium on Genetics, Paleontology, and Evolution," in *Genetics, Paleontology, and Evolution*, edited by Jepson, Mayr, and Simpson, Princeton University Press, Princeton, 1949, pp. 423, 424.

6. Morrison, Thomas F., Frederick D. Cornett, and J. Edward Tether, *Human Physiology*, Henry Holt and Company, New York, 1959, p. 366.

LESSON 11
ADAPTATION — NATURAL SELECTION

Scripture: Job 38:39-41; Prov. 6:6-8; Prov. 30:24-31; Song of Solomon 2:11-13, 15-17. The books of poetry in the Old Testament contain several references to living things in their natural home.

Most evolutionists of today accept some form or variation of Darwin's theory of how new species arose. New forms (mutations) appeared. Immediately natural selection was brought to bear on the different forms. Some were better adapted to survive and reproduced more of their kind. Those less well fitted to the environment died. With changing environment forms changed. This is called by Darwin "survival of the fittest." To summarize: new forms spontaneously appeared and then those best adapted to the environment were preserved while the less well adapted died. This happened successively so that the many species known today finally, over the course of millions of years, evolved.

The evolution of the horse can be taken as an example. The small animal supposed to be the ancestor of the modern horse is thought to have lived in a moist forest. It was a browser eating soft leaves. Its teeth were low crowned and soft. As millions of years passed the climate changed to a dryer one and grasses became more abundant. Horses then evolved the high-crowned hard teeth better adapted to grazing and chewing the hard grasses. Over the years horses' teeth varied (mutations again). Those with the harder teeth could chew the grasses better so they survived and passed on the harder teeth to their offspring. The horses with softer teeth were handicapped and eventually disappeared.

EVOLUTION OF HORSE

Supposedly the horses' long legs and hoofs evolved at the same time in a similar way. The three or four toed feet were adapted to walking on the soft ground of the moist forests. When dry grasslands replaced the forests the hard hooves replaced the toes which could not endure the hard ground. Simultaneously the legs became longer because horses had to run fast on the open plains to escape predators instead of hiding among the leaves in the forest. The longer legged horses escaped their enemies and passed longer legs on to their offspring while the shorter legged animals got caught and killed and could not pass on the shorter legs.

The Biotic Community

The plants and animals living together in one area comprise what is called a *biotic community*. Such a community may be quite large such as a continent. Within a *macrocommunity* (large community) may be found other macrocommunities. For example in North America are found the Canadian Arctic, Canadian and Central United States grasslands, coniferous forests of northeastern United States and southern Canada, deciduous forests of eastern United States, the southwestern desert, and the mountain ranges. These large communities are successively divided into smaller communities until we reach the *microcommunity* (small community). A microcommunity may be only one tree or bush or it may be a small pond.

The *habitat* is where an organism lives within a community. A pond is one kind of habitat, a grassy area another one, and a woodland still another.

The work of an organism within a habitat is called a *niche*. For example on the prairies of Texas are commonly seen certain birds. On the ground are meadowlarks and bobwhite quails. The quails eat seeds while the meadowlark eats insects. They occupy different niches. There is overlapping to some extent; the quail eats some insects, too. The scissortail flycatcher also eats insects but it catches them in the air. It belongs to another niche. The sparrowhawk eats large insects such as grasshoppers and mice. The redtailed hawk eats rodents and smaller birds. In the same area the turkey vulture eats carrion. All of these birds live in the same community but they occupy different niches.

The biotic community always is made up of certain classifications of organisms according to their work or the niches they occupy. The basis of a community are the food producers or plants. In a prairie community a variety of grasses with some weeds make up the food producers. In a woodland trees and shrubs are the food producers. In a pond or stream the algae produce food. Each community is named according to the most numerous plants. There are grasslands, deciduous forests, or coniferous forests.

The herbivores or plant eaters are animals which eat plants. They range from insects to cows or horses. Rabbits are herbivores found in the grassland or the woodland while squirrels are found only in woodland where they eat nuts or acorns. In the pond tiny protozoa, worms, and minute baby fish or other animals are herbivores eating the algae.

Carnivores or animal eaters eat herbivores or other carnivores.

Parasites are organisms that live on other organisms without killing them. Cows or rabbits have ticks living on them while in the pond leeches may attack fish or turtles.

Scavengers are organisms that remove dead matter from the earth or water. Some insects, earthworms, pond snails, crayfish, and turkey vultures are scavengers.

The decomposers are bacteria, molds, and other fungi which bring about the decay of dead organisms. By this means the organisms are removed from the earth and converted to fertilizer for the soil.

Each type of habitat has specific animals or plants for specific jobs. Let us take insectivores (insect eating animals) as an example. We already have mentioned the quail and meadowlark as insectivores on the grassland. Towhees and thrashers perform a similar function in forests. By the edge of the pond frogs eat insects and in the water small fish consume insect larvae while some fish leap out of the water to snap up insects at the surface. There are woodland flycatchers and the scissortails on the prairie doing the same work. Other woodland insectivores are the chickadees, tiny birds which remove insects from leaves and twigs. Insects on the trunks and large branches are destroyed by nuthatches while woodpeckers eat the grubs and beetles inside the wood. Each of these insectivores occupies a specific niche.

In each community will be found relationships called food chains. The basis of each chain will be plants whether land plants or algae in the water. Using the prairie as an example, we find insects eat the plants. The insects in turn are eaten by quails while the quails will be consumed by hawks. In the pond algae are eaten by very small animals which in turn are eaten by small fish and then they are used as food by the larger fish. Always in order in the chain are plants—herbivores—carnivores. Not only do food chains indicate a complexity of the biotic community but we find much interdependence. That is, organisms must have each other to get along. In the western part of the United States are many yuccas, plants with dagger-like leaves and tall stalks with many white bell-shaped flowers. These flowers depend entirely on a small white moth to carry the pollen from flower to flower and pollinate them. The moth gathers a small ball of the pollen and pushes it down into the pistil of the flower. Then she lays her eggs in the side of the ovary of the flower. The pollen fertilizes the seeds making them grow. The moth larvae eat part but not all of the seeds. The remaining seeds scatter and produce more plants. Neither moth nor yucca could exist without the other. Many other examples could be given but this will suffice.

Evolution and the Biotic Community

Returning to our earlier study of genetics we learned that mutations occur. It is believed by the evolutionist that the environment then determines whether or not the mutation is passed on or dies. If it is passed on then a slight change in the organism has taken place. A succession of slight changes resulted in the many forms known today.

It is believed that through the ages many changes have taken place in the earth's surface. As those changes occurred new niches were produced. Then the organisms best adapted to each niche moved in. With successive changes they became better adapted. Then when another change in environment occurred still more changes took place. As mutations occurred the forms best adapted survived and filled the new niches.

Using birds as an example we find some live on the ground. They have strong feet but they usually don't fly as well as many other forms. However, ground dwellers don't all occupy the same niche. Insect eaters like the meadowlark have a relatively small or slender bill but such birds as the quail have stronger beaks which enable them to eat weed seeds which are harder. The flycatchers moved into the niche made up of flying insects. They have strong wings but their feet are used only for perching so they are relatively weak. Likewise the hawk evolved large feet with hooked talons and beaks made for tearing meat. In each case as slight mutations supposedly happened the best adapted for each niche survived. Thus many forms eventually evolved. The developing of forms to live in each of the many niches is referred to as *adaptation*. The action of the environment in bringing about the changes is called *natural selection*.

Let us explain it this way. Supposedly all these birds evolved from a common, that is the same, ancestor. From one clutch of eggs that hatched one bird had a larger beak than the others. Since the beak was stronger it could eat larger insects. One of its offspring had a still larger beak, perhaps with a small hook on it. Its feet were stronger, too, so it could and did eat mice. Descendants of these birds had successively larger beaks and stronger feet until the modern hawk evolved. They were able to eat rodents such as rabbits, so they live in that niche. Similarly other birds evolved small beaks which enabled them to eat small insects. In short an organism lives in a certain niche because it evolved structures adapted to that niche, not because it evolved the structure in order to fit the niche. This is called *postadaptation*. It is believed by some evolutionists that some organisms evolved certain structures which were of little value at the time but were ready to be used when the environment changed. This is called *preadaptation*.

The Long Days Theory and Ecology

Previously we discussed the theory describing the "days" of Genesis as long periods of time. From this lesson we have learned how very complex the living world is. Plants were created on the third day while the sun, moon, and stars were created on the fourth day. On the fifth day water animals and birds were created with land animals being placed on the earth the sixth day. If the days were millions of years long, how could the plants live long periods in darkness since each day consisted of evening and morning? Also, how did the plants which depend on insects for pollination get along without bees? In a balanced habitat the organisms depend on each other. How could this relationship exist if the days were long periods of time?

Problems for the Evolutionist

There are many problems for the evolutionist which he finds difficult to answer. Using a pond as an example, let us first consider the complexity of a biotic community or habitat. The algae provide food for small animals such as protozoa and small crustaceans. These organisms in turn are eaten by small fish. These are then eaten by larger fish. There are different kinds of fish. Minnows are surface feeders while catfish feed on the bottom of the pond. Dead animals and plants sink to the bottom where they are consumed by scavengers such as snails and crayfish. Bacteria decay part of the material returning minerals to the water. Tadpoles are vegetarian, eating algae but adult frogs eat insects and other small animals. Dragon flies hover over the water catching mosquitoes while the young of both live in the water. A turtle paddles its way across the water ready to snap up a fish or frog. This only briefly describes the pond. Food producers, herbivores, carnivores, scavengers — all are supposed by the theory to have evolved.

Evolution is a theory arrived at by observations of many kinds. There are many questions which can't reasonably be answered according to evolution. One of the simplest is how did so many organisms manage to evolve at the same time and keep a perfectly balanced pond? If life began as one cell and from that cell all of these forms arose, how did so many different forms arise? Why did they not all just remain cells?

In short, how could chance produce such a beautifully balanced community of living things? How did all of them evolve at just the right rate?

Teleology is a term applied to the idea that there is a cause or directive force bringing about an effect. The Christian is a teleologist when he believes God is the originator of the highly complex natural world. God is the force and the natural world is the effect. It is easier to believe in a Supreme Being who ordered the universe than to believe the vast number of living things came about as a result of random changes.

Summary

According to evolutionary theory the many kinds of organisms have arisen by means of mutations which were preserved by natural selection. As changes in environment occurred new niches were formed. Those niches were filled by the organisms which already possessed characteristics permitting them to survive (preadaptation) or were able to evolve such traits (postadaptation). The biotic community is so complex that it is hard to believe that all the living things just chanced to evolve at exactly the rate necessary to keep the balance. If it takes thousands of years for just one successful mutation to occur in one organism, the number of mutations necessary to evolve a complete interdependent community becomes astronomical. There is such a fine interdependence in the natural world with each kind of organism taking its place making life possible for other organisms while it pursues its own life, it is hard to imagine a cut-throat existence among living things producing such an intricate world. The complexity must have been planned by a Creator.

SUGGESTED ACTIVITIES

1. Explain how the complexity of the living world provides an argument against the theory of evolution.

----

2. Explain how this complexity provides an argument against the Long Days Theory.

----

3. What is meant by adaptation?

....

....

....

4. Explain natural selection.

....

....

....

5. Can adaptation and natural selection explain variation within a species?

....

....

....

....

6. Name three birds found in yards, vacant lots, or on church grounds. Give the niche of each.

Bird	Niche
a...	....
b...	....
c...	....

7. Let the class take a hike through a woods or by a roadside. Let the students compete finding evidences of complexity of relationship among the living things observed.

8. On the bulletin board post pictures found in magazines illustrating complex relationships. Find pictures illustrating variation.

9. Find evidences of variation in plants in the students' yards. Size and shape of leaves; variations, in color, number of petals, shape of petals, presence of fragrance in flowers; type of growth (stocky, tall, bushy); and other traits can be studied. Try to decide whether the variations are due to differences in heredity or whether environment (temperature, water, etc.) caused variations. Try to group the plants according to what may have been the original created "kinds."

LESSON 12
MISCELLANEOUS CONSIDERATIONS

Scripture: I Jno. 4:12; Rom. 11:33; I Jno. 5:20. We can not
   see God, and we can not understand Him, but Jesus revealed Him to us and we know Him by faith.

The Need for a Basic Philosophy

In this lesson several very important general principles
will be considered. It is impossible for one person to understand all phases of the Bible-evolution conflict. Also, rapidly
changing scientific ideas would necessitate constant study to
keep one's understanding and knowledge current. The Christian
needs some basic understandings to undergird his faith and enable him to meet new theories and so-called evidences that so
frequently appear in print. It is not a matter of being able to
answer every argument but of having a broad philosophical
basis for one's faith. A Bible-centered, rock-like faith is not
moved by drifting tides and dashing waves of hypotheses,
theories, and opinions of man.

The Basis of All Truth—God

God is the basis of all truth. As a freshman in college
this writer heard a fine teacher make this statement: "Science
and the Bible do not conflict. Theory and theology sometimes
do conflict." Theory is man's opinion about what God created.
Since man lacks much knowledge, his theories are subject to

error. Theology is Man's opinion about the Bible. Since Man can not understand all the Bible and also because his study methods may be faulty, Man's opinions may be wrong. So when there appear to be conflicts the trouble lies in faulty theory or theology or both. The Bible is God's revealed word and therefore is perfect. God created the universe. There can be no conflict between God's revelation and His creation. God is truth.

Can't Prove God or Bible by Science

Neither God nor the Bible can be proved by science. The evidence of God as seen in the complexity of the universe is a priori evidence, not empirical evidence. There is no way to set up an experiment which would prove or disprove God. If God is, He is everywhere. There could be no control where God is not to check against the experiment designed to determine whether or not He is.

Archeology is a valuable science often used as evidence of the truth of the Bible. The science provides evidence of the historical accuracy of scripture but it does not prove the inspiration of the Book. Archeological evidence itself is subject to error since archeologists can not always be sure of their interpretation of their findings.

God is His own proof of His deity. He proves Himself through His dealings with Man and that proof is revealed to us through the Bible. If the Bible is an inspired Book then God is. The proofs of the inspiration of the Bible are not part of this course but are left for other courses.

Not uncommonly there is some news report of a scientist who finds evidence of God in his work. His teleological evidence suggests a Supreme Being or an Intelligence that ordered the universe. Often the scientist will prove to be an evolutionist. The evidence he uses suggests an Intelligence but does not reveal God as a Kind Father nor does it reveal Jesus as His Son.

Scientific Method Can't be Used to Prove Evolution

Another discrepancy in the theory of evolution lies in the fact that it can't be verified by scientific experimentation. For this reason it can not be considered a law but must be called a theory or better still an hypothesis. There is no way to experiment with evolution of the past, and present evolution, if there is such, would be too slow for experimentation. Scientists have experimented with fruit flies for many years, but have not produced a new genus. If a new genus should be produced it still would not be evidence that the major categories changed in the past.

Difficulties on Both Sides

There are difficulties for both creationists and evolutionists in this problem. Let us consider the fossils and geology. We have discussed problems for the evolutionists such as the missing links. But neither can creationists answer all the puzzling facts of geology. The flood alone does not provide a simple answer.

Christians need not be concerned because many questions can't be answered. God did not reveal the facts and man has no way of finding out. He only can theorize.

THERMODYNAMICS
...a running down process

theory of EVOLUTION
...a building up process

The Second Law of Thermodynamics

One of the basic principles of physics is the Second Law of Thermodynamics. Stated in simple terms the law merely means the universe is running down. It is wearing out. Heat always is dissipated. A hot object always becomes cooler unless heat energy is being brought in from some outside source. The stars are losing their heat energy and if time should last long enough they would become cold bodies. When a piece of wood burns the heat energy passes into space and can never be recovered for use, though it has not been destroyed. The wood itself is converted into other materials and can never be wood again. A watch never winds itself but always runs down. Water always runs downhill, never uphill. Chemicals tend to break apart to simpler materisls rather than to become more complex. The physicist knows no exception to this law.

According to the evolutionary hypothesis simple molecules of matter arrange themselves into living sells. Then cells differentiated and eventually formed higher organisms. Evolutionists do not believe life is originating now but that organisms of today are continuing to evolve. This implies a continued increase in complexity of matter which is directly opposed to the Second Law of Thermodynamics.

There is abundant empirical evidence to support the law of physics while the hypothesis of evolution depends entirely on a priori reasoning. The evidence for evolution is subjective evidence. That is, it is a matter of personal interpretation on the part of the individual. Such opinions are influenced by the personal bias of the individual. It is more logical to accept a well founded law which does not conflict with scripture in any way than to accept an unproved hypothesis which does conflict with the Bible.

Attitudes of Christians Toward Science

Christians recognize the importance of science and respect the work of scientists. In Gen. 1:28 God told Adam to "Be fruitful and multiply, and replenish the earth, and subdue it: and have dominion over the fish of the sea, and over the fowl of the air, and over every living thing that moveth upon the earth." When man uses the natural world he is obeying God's command to subdue the earth. The scientist learns how to subdue the earth. True science is a blessing to man. It is theories or hypothesis about the living world which conflict with God's revelation to which Christians object.

Although we do not always agree with their philosophy we do respect evolutionary scientists for their research methods and their attempts to be objective or open minded. Scientists regard religion as outside their study. They do not attempt to explain the soul. However, both science and scripture deal with origins. Since the evolutionist attempts to explain origins on a completely materialistic basis and scripture ascribes the origin of the universe and of life to supernatural source, the two philosophies conflict. Many evolutionists are sincere in their convictions. We respect their sincerity while we disagree with their beliefs. It should be remembered that not all scientists are evolutionists but that many fine scientists are creationists.

Can a Christian Believe in Evolution?

The answer to this question is, "Yes" and "No". Yes, a Christian can accept the limited evolution or changes that apparently have taken place in the lower categories. There are wide variations in some species and even genera show variations.

The second answer is given to the theory that life started in some ocean and forms changed until Man appeared. Often when students are being taught this idea the teacher will suggest that God created the living world by evolution. That is to satisfy the student who has been taught the Bible. The leading evolutionists do not believe it. Neither can Christians believe it. If Man evolved, then there is no point at which he became in the image of God or received a soul. There is no sin, the Garden of Eden, and a promise of a Savior. There would be no sacrifice of Jesus and plan of salvation. If life evolved there would be no truth to the Bible.

According to scripture Man is a fallen being in need of salvation. He is dependent on God for his soul's needs. According to evolutionary theory Man represents the highest form of life and is self sufficient. His capacity to evolve is considered his greatest hope for the future. This is a very bleak outlook compared to the Christian's hope of eternal salvation with the Great God in Heaven and the Lord and Savior, Jesus Christ.

Some Results of Accepting Evolution

Aside from losing faith in the Bible there are some other results of accepting evolution.

According to organic evolution, Man is a highly evolved animal, a highly special animal, but still an animal. Animals are amoral. That is, they are neither moral or immoral. If man is an animal, should he not behave as an animal? Could that be the basis of much of the immorality of today?

Organic evolutionists believe that Man now has the power to direct his own evolution. They, also, believe that should be his highest aim. Several ways have been proposed to produce this superman. One is to prevent the "unfit" from becoming parents. Another is to encourage the "fit" to have more children. This brings up a question. Who is to decide who is "fit" or who is "unfit?" Still another way is to control crossing or to decide who is to be father of a child. This destroys the sanctity of the home and the sacredness of marriage.

The organic evolutionist does not anticipate Heaven. With no hope of a future life, what incentive is there to live a life such as Christians live?

Life in Nazi Germany or Communist Russia illustrates what happens when atheism is the controlling philosophy. People are considered of no value. Human suffering means nothing. In Russia evolution is one of the official philosophies of the nation.

Evolution Unnecessary to Biology

It is claimed by modern evolutionists that biology can't be understood without evolution. That is not true. It can be explained this way. The appendix is considered a vestigial organ and is one evidence that man evolved from an animal which used its appendix. It is not necessary for a doctor to know about this theory in order to diagnose appendicitis and remove the appendix. The heart specialist does not have to know the stages in supposed heart evolution to treat the patient. The treatment is based on what the heart is like now, not on what it may have been like some time in the past. The plant breeder works with Mendel's Laws, not evolution, when he produces improved squashes or beans. There is no process in nature which one can't understand without evolution.

It is said, too, that evolution is the great unifying principle in biology. Structural and chemical similarities of organisms are supposed to indicate common origin and unity. Isn't it just as simple to say God created them on similar patterns? And besides that, is it necessary to consider nature unified? God created things separately.

Taxonomists (those who name plants and animals) claim organisms can't be classified without an understanding of their evolution. But their supposed evolution is arrived at by studying their structure. The creationist will say the lions and tigers belong to the Felidae and the dogs and wolves belong to the Canidae because lions and tigers are more like each other than they are like the cats while the lions and tigers belong to the Felidae because they resemble each other more than they do the Canidae. The evolutionists will state the animals are classified as they are because of their evolutionary history. In both cases structure is the basis for the classification. Some of the early taxonomists did not accept evolution. Linnaeus, the father of modern taxonomy, was a creationist.

VITALIST...
believes extra "something" in living matter

MECHANIST...
believes living matter simply chemical

Vitalism Versus Mechanism

The vitalist believes there is some kind of factor other than physical and chemical factors involved in living matter. The vitalists of the Middle Ages went so far as to believe that living processes could not be explained by man. In time

98

scientists began to discover that many living processes are chemical changes and that chemicals in the body behave just like they do outside the body. Then many scientists adopted the opposite extreme. They believed all life processes are purely chemical and physical in nature and there is no vital principle involved. Those accepting this philosophy are called materialists or mechanists. They do not recognize any factor other than natural law. In other words they deny God has any part in the natural world. The organic evolutionists of today are mechanists.

The Christian recognizes that body functions are chemical in their nature but he doesn't stop there. He realizes there is an extra "something" involved in living matter. The work of the digestive system may be used as an example. The digestive juices in the stomach chemically change certain foods. This digestion can take place in a test tube as well as in the stomach. But the enzymes were produced by living cells which were able to select necessary materials from the blood and combine them to make the digestive juice. These cells are affected by one's emotions. Anger or fear stop the process while happy emotions stimulate the formation of juices. Thus we see the production of juices is more than simple chemistry. This is vitalism. Not all vitalists are Christians. Christians accept mechanism to the extent that physical and chemical principles in living matter are recognized but in addition the Christian believes in God as the vitalistic force which created the living matter and enabled it to carry on life processes.

Mechanists explain human behavior on the basis of organic evolution. Man's behavior results from his animal ancestry, they say. Aside from its spiritual implications, this philosophy can have serious results. Let us put it this way; if man feels that he is only an evolved animal, will he not behave like an animal? He will lose his moral standards and will have no regard for the rights of others. If he believes in Darwin's doctrine of the survival of the fittest, he will have no respect for minority groups or down trodden individuals. The Nazi's showed that philosophy when they tried to exterminate the Jews as well as other supposedly "unfit" peoples. The mechanist has no hope of a reward in heaven. With no expectation of a reward there is no incentive to live according to Christian standards.

Some Basic Principles

While this material was in preparation periodicals came to the writer's desk with articles about new discoveries. Two articles were about recently discovered fossils which were thought possibly to be man's ancestors. Another article was about a new chemical produced in a laboratory which some believe confirms Oparin's theory of the origin of life. None of the articles affected the accuracy of these lessons. New discoveries such as these are frequent. There will be still others by the time this material is in print.

Obviously it is impossible to try to explain every such discovery in the light of scripture. First no one person can possibly know enough science to be able to explain all the theories. Then the theories constantly are changing. To meet this constant stream of material the young Christian needs a basic philosophy or a basic set of principles that will enable him to retain his faith regardless of what science says or of what attacks may be made on the Bible. Following is a summary of such basic principles:

1. God revealed Himself to Man through His dealings with him. The Bible is the record of those dealings.

2. The Bible is not a book of science. The science found in the Book is incidental, but since the Bible is true the science found in it is accurate and true.

3. The Bible can be neither proved nor disproved by science.

4. Some science, especially archeology, helps confirm the historical accuracy of the Bible but such external evidence merely contributes to the internal evidence.

5. The Bible is unchanging. Science constantly is changing.

6. Man's understanding of the universe is very imperfect. This being true, beliefs about the universe often are erroneous.

7. It is not necessary to be able to answer all evolutionary arguments to have a firmly established faith in scripture.

8. Any apparent conflict of science and scripture should be viewed with an open mind remembering that Man's understanding of scripture and of science are subject to error, and also remembering that the Bible has stood the test of time as an inspired, true revelation of God.

9. It is impossible to understand some parts of the Bible. For example the term "kinds" can not be defined in terms of modern classifications.

10. It is possible for people to have different ideas as to the meaning of certain parts of the account of the creation and still accept the inspiration of the Book. It is true that theistic evolutionists will take a statement such as this and use it to support their contention that God created by evoluion, but they will be hard pressed to take the simple account of Genesis and turn it into evolution over eons of time.

SUGGESTED ACTIVITIES

1. List some of the reasons why one should establish basic reasons for one's faith rather than try to answer every argument presented by evolutionists.

a. ....

b. ....

c. ....

2. The Bible can neither be proved nor disproved by science. Explain this statement.

....

....

....

....

....

....

3. What would be the results if our faith in the Bible had to depend on scientific verification?

....

....

....

....

....

....

4. Prepare a list of theories concerning some phase of evolution which are not mentioned in this book. Recent text books, library books, periodicals, and newspapers with recent copyright dates should supply material.

5. Let members of the class prepare special reports on recent theories or discoveries which have a bearing on evolutionary theory.

6. Discuss ways in which the theories can be refuted. The class might enjoy preparing a debate on one of the subjects.

REVIEW

SUGGESTIONS: Teacher and students should fill out all blanks before coming to class. The material covers the high points of each lesson. Try to summarize the chief ideas of the course. Additional material for discussion might be brought up. (Ex. Recent newspaper or magazine articles, recent experiences of the student in the classroom, or a TV or radio program). Make the review snappy and lively. Definite topics or lessons might be assigned for special reports.

REVIEW LESSON

LESSON 1—INTRODUCTION

1. State the two common beliefs concerning the origin of the universe and of life.

   a. _____

   b. _____

2. Define the following terms:

   a. Theistic evolution: _____

   _____

   b. Organic evolution: _____

   _____

3. Give two reasons why one should study evolution.

   a. _____

   _____

   b. _____

   _____

LESSON 2—ORIGIN OF THE UNIVERSE

1. What fact about the beginning of the universe does science seldom attempt to explain? _____

_____

2. On what basis do creationists "understand that the world was created by the word of God?" _____

_____

LESSON 3—THE ORIGIN OF LIFE

1. Name two problems concerning origins which evolutionists are studying.

    a. ....

    b. ....

2. State the discrepancy between the Law of Biogenesis and evolutionary theory concerning the origin of life..........................

....

....

LESSON 4—THE ORIGIN OF MAN

1. List the three basic forms of man as found in the fossil record.

    a...   b...

    c...

2. Explain why reconstructions of the fossils are so often unreliable.

....

....

....

3. Explain where the major gap in Man's supposed evolutionary lineage is found.

....

....

....

LESSON 5—DATES AND TIME

1. List three reasons why the date 4004 B. C. likely is not the date of Adam's creation.

    a. ....

    b. ....

    c. ....

2. Give three reasons why the date of original creation can't be determined.

a. ....

b. ....

c. ....

3. List five reasons why radioactive dating is not dependable.

a. ....

b. ....

c. ....

d. ....

e. ....

4. Explain why we should not be concerned about the apparent discrepancy between Biblical dates and scientific dates...............

....

....

....

LESSON 6—CLASSIFICATION AND THE EVOLUTIONARY TREE

1. The term "kind" used in Genesis has been confused with the term "species" used by scientists. Explain how this has resulted in misunderstandings.

....

....

....

....

2. What important fact in the fossil record suggests that all organisms always have been in separate groups?.....................

....

....

....

LESSON 7—FOSSILS AND THE AGES

1. Explain the basis for the divisions of time in the so-called geological column. ....

....

....

....

2. List three irregularities in the assumed sequence of fossils in strata.

    a. ....

    b. ....

    c. ....

3. How do the gaps in the fossil record provide an explanation of the "kinds" of Genesis. ....

....

....

....

LESSON 8—GEOLOGY AND THE FLOOD

1. Explain the difference between uniformitarianism and catastrophism.

....

....

....

....

2. List three things scripture does not reveal about the flood.

    a. ....

    b. ....

    c. ....

3. List three evidences that the fossils were formed as a result of catastrophic burial in a flood.

    a. ....

    b. ....

    c. ....

4. How does fossil evidence suggest the world once was very different?

----

5. How does scripture suggest a different world before the flood?

LESSON 9—PHYSICAL EVIDENCE

1. How does the creationist explain the similarity of structure observed in various classes of animals?----------------------------------

----

2. List three so-called evidences of evolution found in embryological development.

    a. --

    b. --

    c. --

3. How does the creationist answer these arguments?----------------

----

----

4. What are vestigial organs and what is their supposed significance?

----

5. How does the creationist explain vestigial organs?----------------

----

LESSON 10—HEREDITY AND EVOLUTION

1. Give two facts about mutations which make them unlikely means of evolution.

   a. ....

   b. ....

2. What two kinds of changes in the germ cell can cause change in an organism?

   a. ....

   b. ....

3. How can the changes man has produced in domesticated organisms be explained?

....

....

....

4. Explain this limited evolution as contrasted with the "molecules to man" sort of evolution..

....

....

....

LESSON 11—ADAPTATION-NATURAL SELECTION

1. Explain how the complexity of a biotic community provides evidence against evolution..

....

....

2. Explain how interdependence in the natural world provides evidence against the Long Day Theory..

....

....

....

3. List some difficult questions for the evolutionist to answer about adaptation and natural selection.

a. ....

b. ....

c. ....

LESSON 12—SOME BASIC PRINCIPLES

1. Explain why evolutionary theory is dangerous to the Christian.

....

....

....

....

2. Explain why one must establish a basic philosophy rather than try to meet every argument of the evolutionist. ....

....

....

....

....

Finishing the Course

As a culmination of this course the class might present a program of some sort teaching others of the dangers of accepting the hypothesis. The elders might allow one or more of the boys to give talks to other classes or to the church at midweek services. The girls could prepare a lesson for the younger children about the creation.

Students with artistic ability could prepare posters for class rooms depicting the creation as contrasted with evolution.

COLLATERAL READING

At the end of each lesson is found a bibliography of works cited in that lesson. Most of them are college (often graduate) level works and were used because it is in such books that suitable documentation can be found for the material in this course. Most of those references are too difficult for those who will be using this book and many of them are evolutionary works. The list of references below is made up of books refuting evolution. Most of the authors are scientists and the science found in the works is quite sound. In some cases the author's theology creeps in. Books especially suitable for young people are marked with an asterisk.

Clark, Robert E. D., *Darwin: Before and After*, Grand Rapids International Publications, Grand Rapids, Michigan, 1958. (192 pp.)

Handrich, Theodore L., *THE CREATION: Facts, Theories, and Faith*, Moody Press, Chicago, 1953. (299 pp.)

Klotz, John W., *Genes, Genesis, and Evolution*, Concordia Publishing House, Saint Louis, 1955. (575 pp.)

Klotz, John W., *Modern Science in the Christian Life*, Concordia Publishing House, Saint Louis, 1961. (191 pp.)

Marsh, Frank Lewis, *Evolution, Creation and Science*, Second Edition, Review and Herald Publishing Association, Washington, D. C., 1947. (381 pp.)

*Marsh, Frank Lewis, *Evolution or Special Creation*, Review and Herald Publishing Association, Washington, D. C., 1963. (64 pp.)

*Morris, Henry M., *The Twilight of Evolution*, The Presbyterian and Reformed Publishing Co., Philadelphia, 1963. (103 pp.)

Nelson, Byron C., *"After Its Kind"*, Augsburg Publishing House, Minneapolis, 1962. (195 pp.)

Rehwinkel, Alfred M., *The Flood*, Concordia Publishing House, Saint Louis, 1951. (371 pp.)

*Riegle, David D., *Creation or Evolution?*, Zondervan Publishing House, Grand Rapids, 1962. (63 pp.)

*Thomas, J. D., *The Doctrine of Evolution and the Antiquity of Man*, Biblical Research Press, Abilene, Texas, 1961. (64 pp.)

Thompson, W. R., "Introduction", *The Origin of Species*, Charles Darwin, *Everyman's Library*, No. 811, Dutton, New York, 1928. (18 pp.)

Whitcomb, John C. Jr., and Henry M. Morris, *The Genesis Flood*, Baker Book House, Grand Rapids, Michigan, 1961. (518 pp.)

Zimmerman, Paul A., Editor, *Darwin, Evolution, and Creation*, Concordia Publishing House, Saint Louis, 1959. (231 pp.)

NOTES